TO ALL WHO ASPIRE

DEVILS TOWER NATIONAL MONUMENT

A Climber's Guide

Steve Gardiner

and

Dick Guilmette

THE MOUNTAINEERS
Seattle

The Mountaineers: Organized 1906 *"... to explore and study the mountains, forests, and watercourses of the Northwest."*

Published by The Mountaineers
306 2nd Avenue West, Seattle, WA 98119

Published simultaneously in Canada by Douglas & McIntyre, Ltd.
1615 Venables St., Vancouver, B.C. V5L 2H1
Manufactured in the United States of America

Edited by Barbara Chasan
Designed by Bridget McNamara
Maps by B. Adams and Newell Cartographics
Cover photos: West Face of the Tower (Dick Guilmette photo) and Steve Gardiner climbing Durrance route (Mark Brackin photo)
Frontispiece: Tower view from the west (Dick Guilmette photo)

Library of Congress Cataloging in Publication Data

Gardiner, Steve.
Devils Tower National Monument.

Includes index.
1. Rock climbing—Wyoming—Devils Tower National Monument—Guide-books. 2. Devils Tower National Monument (Wyo.)—Guide books. I. Guilmette, Dick. II. Title.
GV199.42.W82D434 1986 917.87'13 86-12408
ISBN 0-89886-120-9

0 9 8 7 6

5 4 3 2 1

CONTENTS

ACKNOWLEDGMENTS

We want to thank the National Park Service and Superintendent Homer Robinson of Devils Tower National Monument for full use of their facilities, records, and photo file. We would also like to thank Terry Rypkema, Curt Haire, Dingus McGee, and the Last Pioneer Woman for their early work in recording climbing events at the Tower.

Bruce Adams did an excellent job of preparing the preliminary topographical and area maps for this book. For carefully reviewing and commenting on the route material prior to publication, we thank Dennis Horning, Hollis Marriott, Todd Skinner, Dave Larsen, Paul Piana, Charlie Anderson, Beth Wald, and Danny Rosen. Donna DeShazo, Barbara Chasan, Ann Cleeland, and Stephen Whitney of The Mountaineers Books were helpful and professional in developing this book. We give a special thanks to park ranger Jim Schlinkmann and Mike Robinson for their interest and time spent researching, typing, and rechecking the route information, and to the many climbers through the years who have submitted route descriptions or commented on route information.

FOREWORD

The main interest of the National Park Service regarding Devils Tower National Monument is in preserving this unique natural wonder at the same time that climbing activity continues. In this vein, the National Park Service commends the thrust of free and clean climbing while allowing the use of pitons where nothing else will suffice. Cooperation between climbers and the National Park Service in the protection of Devils Tower National Monument will ensure the everlasting challenge of this excellent climbing area.

Homer A. Robinson
Superintendent
Devils Tower National Monument

Todd Skinner leading first ascent of Animal Cracker Land (Route 48), 1984 (Beth Wald photo)

INTRODUCTION

Devils Tower has become very popular as a climber's destination. During a typical day, one can see parties of climbers on all sides of the Tower. It is possible to meet people from various parts of the United States and many countries of the world.

There is a reason for this interest in the Tower. The columnar jointing which occurred as the molten rock cooled created near-vertical walls and a variety of crack sizes that provide years of challenge for many climbers.

More than 3000 climbs are made on this monolith each year, with 1200 to 1700 climbers reaching the summit. Another 200,000 to 300,000 people come to visit Devils Tower National Monument each year. For some, the urge to try climbing is overwhelming in spite of handicaps. One blind man made a strong attempt, a man with a wooden leg reportedly has been to the top, and a couple brought their justice of the peace to the summit and were married there.

Because Devils Tower is such a quality climbing area and because so many climbers and visitors have requested more climbing information, we have put this book together in a format that will be useful as a comprehensive guide to climbing at Devils Tower and will also give enough of the climbing history so that each reader can sense how climbing has developed here. Some unique events have taken place and they add color to an already interesting piece of rock.

To keep this guide up-to-date and to facilitate a revision should one be necessary in the future, we ask that all climbers who put up new routes or who free climb existing aid routes submit written descriptions of their activities to a ranger or the superintendent prior to leaving the area. A New Route Description Checklist is available for you to fill out. A sketch or photo of the climb showing important points would be appreciated.

Welcome to the Tower. Good climbing!

PART ONE

General Information

CREATION OF DEVILS TOWER NATIONAL MONUMENT

In a presidential proclamation dated September 24, 1906, Theodore Roosevelt declared that "the lofty and isolated rock in the State of Wyoming, known as the 'Devils Tower,' situated upon the public lands owned and controlled by the United States is such an extraordinary example of the effect of erosion in the higher mountains as to be a natural wonder and an object of historic and great scientific interest and it appears that the public good would be promoted by reserving this tower as a National monument."

Roosevelt, using the power of the Act for the Preservation of American Antiquities, set aside Devils Tower as America's first national monument. To declare the rock a national park would have taken an act of Congress, and rumors were around that people in the area were interested in the rocks surrounding the tower for use in building and as souvenirs. Roosevelt, not wanting to take the time for a Congressional act, and following the requests of Wyoming Representative Frank W. Mondell, reportedly chose the quicker method of protecting the area to warn "unauthorized persons not to appropriate, injure, or destroy any feature of the natural tower." The proclamation also prohibited settling or living on any of the lands within the boundary of the monument.

REACHING THE TOWER

The majority of visitors to Devils Tower National Monument will find it easiest to arrive via Interstate 90. If approaching from the east, leave

Opposite: Beth Wald rappelling after first ascent of Avalon, Route 108 (Todd Skinner photo)

Interstate 90 at Sundance and follow Highway 14 to Devils Tower Junction where the route is clearly marked. From the west, leave the Interstate at Moorcroft and continue north to Devils Tower Junction. Both routes are well-marked all the way to the Tower, which is five miles north of Devils Tower Junction.

Visitors who approach the Tower from the north will take Highway 112 through Hulett and Highway 24 south to Devils Tower. Drivers approaching from the south will find that roads lead either to Moorcroft or Sundance, and they can follow the first two routes from those locations.

Commercial airports are at Gillette to the west and Spearfish and Rapid City to the east; however, all three towns are far enough from Devils Tower that flying is not a practical means of reaching the Tower. No bus connections are available to the Tower and hitchhiking, though possible, will be very slow because of the lack of traffic on area highways. It is therefore recommended that visitors wishing to see Devils Tower have their own transportation.

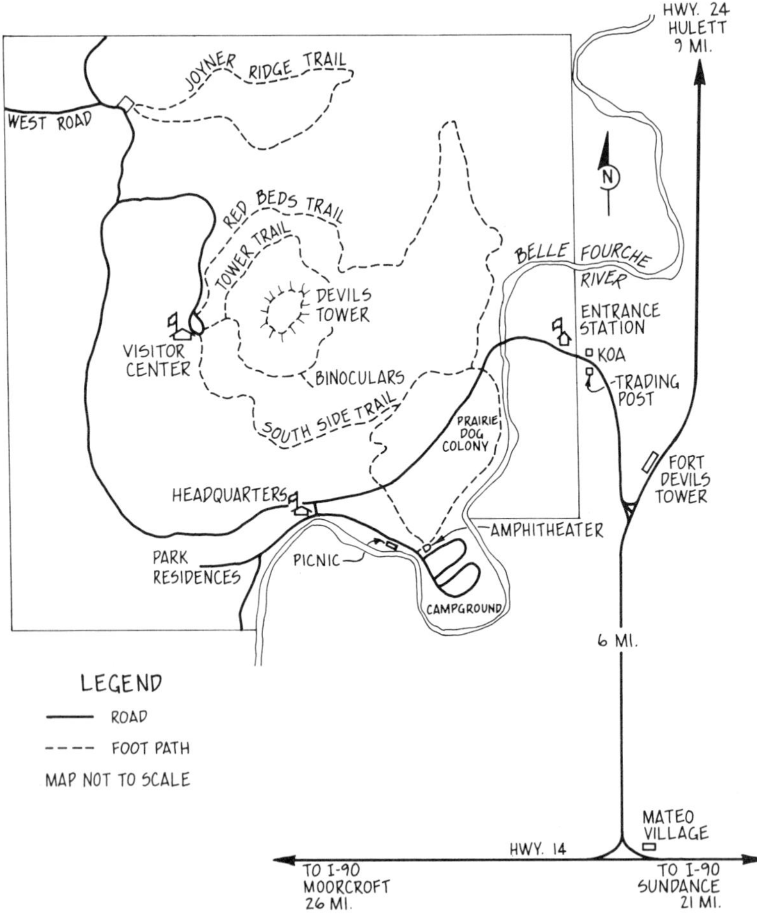

GENERAL REGULATIONS

Everyone must pay a nominal entrance fee to the Monument and a camping fee if they wish to stay overnight when fees are being collected. Information regarding fees and camping is available at the entrance station, from a ranger, or by writing the superintendent, Devils Tower National Monument, Devils Tower, WY 82714. Camping is permitted only in the campground and not on the Tower itself.

Climbers must register with a ranger prior to climbing and must sign in after completing a climb. No commercial climbing is allowed. All accidents and injuries must be reported to a ranger.

Vehicles must comply with all state and federal regulations. Driving a motor vehicle off the park roads is prohibited. Riding bicycles on trails or cross-country is not permitted.

No weapons may be visible in the Monument. This includes guns, bows, slingshots, and BB guns. No littering is allowed (carry everything off the Tower). No alcoholic beverages (open containers) may be possessed on the main park road, in the Visitor Center parking area, or on the Tower Trail. No ground fires are permitted unless under a special-use permit signed by the superintendent. Pets must be physically restrained (leash, cage, etc.) at all times.

WILDLIFE

Hunting is not allowed inside the Monument and various forms of wildlife can be seen at any time of the day or night. These animals, when left alone, do not seem to mind the curious gaze of park visitors and can be easily photographed.

One may see prairie dogs, deer, wild turkey, chipmunks, squirrels, rabbits, porcupines, and an occasional fox, bobcat, bull snake (nonpoisonous), or rattlesnake (poisonous). The rattlesnake can be found in prairie dog holes and in the rocks surrounding the Tower.

The sky belongs to the bald and golden eagles, turkey vulture, red-tailed hawk, goshawk, merlin, and sparrow hawk. The upper sections of Devils Tower are home for rock doves. These are preyed upon by prairie falcons that nest on the Tower. When they have young, these falcons will attack climbers who approach their nests. Attacks have occurred mostly on the west face and occasionally on the north face. Wild turkey, audubon warblers, hairy woodpeckers, western flycatchers, black-capped chickadees, great horned owls, mountain bluebirds, and numerous sparrows are some of the other birds that live in the Monument.

For your own safety and for the health of wildlife, the National Park Service asks that you do not feed or disturb wildlife and allow the animals some space for themselves.

GEOLOGY

Devils Tower rises 1270 feet above the Belle Fourche River to an elevation of 5117 feet. From the talus slope at its base the tower rises approximately 600 feet. Its base diameter is about 800 feet. The top of the tower is relatively flat, with the high point at the center. The summit measures 300 feet across from north to south, and 180 feet from east to west.

During the Cretaceous Period, some 80 million years ago, dinosaurs roamed the Devils Tower region, and the weather and plants were subtropical. Over millions of years, the land sunk and rose several times. Large inland seas covered the region during the episodes of subsidence, only to drain away as the land rose once again. Sediments deposited in those ancient seas hardened to form the widespread horizontal layers of sandstone, shale, gypsum, and siltstone that today surround Devils Tower. The last of these great seas was drained by the Black Hills uplift, which most geologists agree occurred sometime after the birth of the Rocky Mountains, about 70 million years ago.

View south from the top of the Tower (Dick Guilmette photo)

Devils Tower formed when molten rock (magma) rose up through the earth to harden either at the surface or just beneath it. This occurred about 54 million years ago. The surrounding sediments were then eroded away to expose the tower we see today. The latest thorough geologic study of the tower suggests that both the Missouri Buttes and Devils Tower are volcanic necks — the lava-filled conduits of extinct volcanoes. The magma hardened in the conduits and was later exposed by erosion. The igneous (once molten) rock that makes up the tower is phonolite porphyry, a very hard rock in which large crystals of white feldspar are embedded in a finer-grained groundmass.

Besides being nearly vertical, Devils Tower is most striking for its large four-, five-, and six-sided columns, which formed as the magma cooled. These columns are four to eight feet in diameter and hundreds of feet long. The cracks separating the columns may run straight for their full lengths or may fuse at the bottom, middle or top. Many cracks run for long distances at a uniform width, and climbers can pick a crack with the width they are most comfortable with; i.e., finger, hand, fist or foot width etc. This plus easy access to many difficult climbs makes Devils Tower a climber's Mecca.

Top of the Tower showing vegetation, and summit marker in upper left (Dick Guilmette photo)

Several Indian tribes have legends about how Devils Tower formed. It seems that long ago several Indian braves (or seven girls, according to another version) were being chased by a huge bear. This bear, who was the king of all the bears, had a very long tail. To escape, the Indians climbed on top of a rock, or tree stump, and prayed to the Great Spirit to save them. Just as the bear was about to get them, the rock, or tree stump, grew and grew until it became the big tower we see today. Angered, the great bear clawed the sides of the tower, making the deep cracks that run up and down its flanks. The Indian braves came back to earth by hanging on to the legs of eagles they called to rescue them. (The seven young girls went up into the sky to become the Pleiades.) The bear was killed, and thereafter, as punishment, the Great Spirit made only short tails on bears.

Opposite: Painting showing Indian legend of how the Tower was formed (National Park Service file photo)

PART TWO

Historical Information

THE NAMING OF DEVILS TOWER

Originally Devils Tower was known as Mateo Tepee or Mato Tipila, depending on the language, by the Indians living in the area. This translated to "Bear Lodge" or "Grizzly Bear Lodge" and was given because the Indians often saw unusual numbers of bears in the area.

The earliest recorded sighting of Devils Tower was made by Lieutenant G. L. Warren in 1858. He led a scientific expedition to the area of Inyan Kara Mountain where he was stopped from entering the Black Hills by Dakota Indians. He did not reach Devils Tower but noted seeing "BEAR'S LODGE and Little Missouri Buttes" by using a "powerful spy-glass."

The following year, General W. F. Raynolds was assigned to explore the Yellowstone and Missouri rivers. On July 19, Raynolds' men reached Bear Lodge and his journal entry describes it as "an isolated rock on the bank of the river, striking from the fact that it rises in a valley. . . ."

Raynolds included a map of his entire route, showing all his camps and the interesting features he found. Bear Lodge rock is shown.

It was nearly 16 years before another explorer noted the Bear Lodge in his journal. Lieutenant Colonel Richard Irving Dodge of the U.S. Army further explored the Black Hills area and visited Bear Lodge. He called the rock:

> An immense obelisk of granite, eight hundred and sixty-seven feet at base, two hundred and ninety-seven feet top, rises one thousand one hundred and twenty-seven feet above its base, and five thousand one hundred feet above tide-water.
>
> Its summit is inaccessible to anything without wings. The sides are fluted and scored by the action of the elements, and immense blocks of granite, split off from the column by frost, are piled in huge, irregular mounds about its base.

Opposite: Tower view from the southwest (Dick Guilmette photo)

> The Indians call this shaft 'The Bad God's Tower,' a name adopted with proper modification, by our surveyors.*

It is not known if this change in name was intentional or not. Perhaps it was a mistake made by an interpreter. Possibly Dodge simply did not like the Bear Lodge name and chose another. How the change came about is unknown, but when Dodge completed his report and maps, he called the rock Devils Tower.

With many people moving into the area at that time, the name Devils Tower became common, and in 1906, when Roosevelt created the first national monument, he used that name. In 1920, Major General H. L. Scott wrote a letter to the Historical Society of Wyoming hoping "that good taste and historical precedent will appeal to the people of Wyoming to give its most remarkable rock its own aboriginal name."

The reaction of Scott was supported by Chief Luther Standing Bear of the Sioux tribe. Standing Bear, in a letter to historian Dick Stone, wrote:

> Col. Dodge was, as were so many white men in meddling with Indian history, wrong in saying the Indians called the place the bad God's tower. The Sioux had no word for Devil, for the devil and hades of the white man had no place in Indian thought. It is much like the changing of the name to the entrance to the Black Hills from Gate of the Buffalo which the Sioux called it to the inelegant term of the white man, Buffalo Gap.

In spite of protestations of Scott, Standing Bear, and others, the name change remained and, right or wrong, Devils Tower National Monument is the official name today.

A GAME OF HIGH STAKES

THE RAREST SIGHT OF A LIFETIME WILL BE OBSERVED
AND THE 4TH OF JULY WILL BE BETTER SPENT AT THE DEVILS TOWER
THAN AT THE WORLD'S FAIR.

That is what readers learned from the posters and bulletins that were dispersed in the spring of 1893 by William Rogers and Willard Ripley. The pair of ranchers were planning a daring (many observers called it foolhardy) attempt to be the first men to stand at the summit of what is now Devils Tower National Monument.

The handbills promised that the observers would see "Old Glory flung to the breeze from the top of the Tower, 800 feet from the ground by Wm. Rogers." In addition, other attractive features were offered, such as: "Plenty to eat and drink on the grounds!... Lots of hay and grain for the horses!" and "Dancing day and night!"

---

*Dodge, Richard Irving, *The Black Hills* (New York, 1876), 95.

Willard Ripley (above) and William Rogers (left) scaled the summit by stake ladder in 1893 (National Park Service file photos)

Apparently the advertisements were successful because estimates of 1000 to 3000 people, unable to resist the excitement, journeyed to see the extravaganza. People traveled the unimproved roads and trails as far as 125 miles on horseback and by wagons.

The idea for the climb has been credited to two sources. One version gives the idea to Colonel Willard Ripley (father of Willard Ripley who made the climb). Since his ranch was north of Devils Tower, Colonel Ripley could see the Tower every day from his porch and wondered what it might be like to stand on top. Being too old to make such a climb, he proposed the idea to his only son.

The other version of the story credits Will Rogers with the idea. He had apparently gone for a horseback ride in 1891 with his brother-in-law G. A. Knowles. Knowles stated that, "Rogers told me that he was 'going to be on top of that tower before three years.' I told him, 'You are going to break your neck, too,' and Bill said, 'No, I won't, but I am going to be up there.'"

Regardless of where the idea originated, the two men agreed to work on it together. According to Newell Joyner, first superintendent of Devils Tower National Monument, the project had a double purpose and the relationship between the two men was one of business. In a letter to John P. Harrington of the Smithsonian Institution, Joyner wrote:

> Rogers and Ripley were two local ranchers. They were not partners in the ranch, merely being partners in this venture. I have always used the term "commercial celebration" to differentiate from a public non-profit picnic, and also to introduce the idea back of their climb. It is granted that the venture was primarily for the purpose of doing something which no one else had ever done. But the year, 1893, was one of hard-times in this agricultural region. At no time in this region which was then just being settled have there been persons so affluent as to finance an undertaking such as the construction of the ladder. This job required most of a month for several men. Naturally Rogers and Ripley saw where they could gain financially by using the proposed climb as the free attraction to a celebration where refreshments, stands, and all amusements were under their control.

In preparation for their climb, Rogers and Ripley had carefully looked over the faces of the Tower. Knowles, who may have witnessed various parts of the project, says that his brother-in-law "first made a big kite which he tried to fly over the Tower and get a string over which he would use to pull a heavier cord over and in that way get a rope over. But he had to give up this idea because he couldn't get a kite high enough to take the first string over. Then he looked for a crevice into which it would be possible to drive pegs and reach the top that way. With the aid of a pair of field glasses he hunted for a long time and finally discovered the crevice in which the ladder was built." This crevice, on the southeast corner, is a continuously open vertical crack between two columns which appeared (to a person standing at the base) to reach the full height of the escarpment. This illusion, caused by foreshortening, would later present a problem to them.

They began work about June 1, 1893, cutting pegs from native oak, ash, and willow. Since the two men were ranchers, not experienced mountain climbers, they planned to use the pegs as rungs for a ladder rather than use alpine climbing techniques. The pegs were cut 24 to 30 inches in length and sharpened on one end so they could be driven and wedged into the deep crack varying from 2 to 4 inches in width.

This was a nervous time for Alice Mae "Dolly" Ripley, wife of Willard. She said, "While the ladder was built the men camped at the Tower and I cooked for them. It was very exciting and I was under an awful strain while my husband was working up there. Everyday when they went to work I didn't know whether they would all come back at night or not, but they always did."

The National Park Service records show the first pegs (which are now gone) were heavy, long, and close together. Higher on the ladder, however, the wooden stakes became lighter, shorter, and farther apart. Speculation about this difference seems to center around either the possibility that wood sources for good pegs near the Tower began to dwindle and the upper stakes had to be carried greater distances, or time was beginning to run short and they wanted to be sure of their success in advance. As the pegs were driven into the rock, they were braced by a wooden strip which turned the separate pegs into a continuous 350-foot ladder.

During the six weeks that they worked on their project, Rogers and Ripley, ages 35 and 28 respectively, experimented with building methods. They made one valuable discovery which was dictated by the nature of the rock. The left-hand column was flat, but on the right side of the crack the rock protruded outward. Willard Ripley, being left-handed, could stand on one stake, lean his right shoulder and hip against the rock, and still have his left arm free to swing his hammer. It was much easier for him than Rogers to wedge the pegs, so Ripley became the primary worker on the actual construction of the stake ladder.

Mrs. Ripley explained the process by saying the men "used a pulley rope and a pulley to get the stakes up to where they were driven into the crevice. Willard Ripley was left handed so he drove all the stakes as they had to be driven with the left hand. He was the one who did most of the work but Rogers got most of the credit. Rogers and Colonel Ripley cut the pegs and pulled them up to Willard who drove them into the crevice."

Though the construction of the ladder was difficult and dangerous, the hardest part was above. The crack containing the ladder ended at a large ledge they called the Bench (now referred to as the Meadows). At the top of the ladder, it was necessary to complete a "difficult move" to attain the Bench. From that level, another 175 feet of scrambling was required to reach the actual summit.

Mrs. Ripley states, "After the ladder was finished Willard went up on top and then he came back down. He was the first to get on top. It was a very hard climb from the top of the Tower. My husband told me that there was nothing on top of the Tower but a little soil and some sage brush."

Although some disagreement exists about which of the two actually stood on top of Devils Tower first, most sources support Mrs. Ripley's statement. The *Frontier Times* wrote:

> Rogers usually is given credit for being the first man to ascend the Tower, but there are those who contend Willard Ripley was first. They base their contention on the fact that the crack in which the ladder was built curved and because Ripley was left-handed it was easier for him to drive the pegs into the crack. He completed the top of the ladder and it is logical that he was first to reach the top, probably before the designated day of July 4th.

Superintendent Joyner wrote on this issue, "I am inclined to the belief that he (Ripley) was actually the first to reach the top and that he did most of the work in the actual construction of the ladder, altho' there are two contending factions and claims."

The detail of who was first may in reality be less important than the fact that the climb was completed. Joyner, in his report for the historical files, allowed his own enthusiasm and respect to show through when he wrote:

> All this procedure can be told in a sentence or two — but imagine the time and patience (and some say, *nerve*) required to accomplish the construction of the 350 foot ladder. These pegs had to be selected, cut, and conveyed to the base of the Tower. At least the last quarter mile no wagon could enter. Then began the somewhat precipitous climb over a talus slope of small rocks which ended in maneuvering along several ledges and up over an eight foot face. Very few people today in attempting to gain the location of the original bottom peg are successful although it is no trick for anyone who knows the route and has a fair amount of nerve.

During the last weeks before July 4, Will Rogers became the business manager of the operation. He handled the advertising for the free attraction and organized a dance as well as food and drink stands, which would provide the profits that he and Ripley would enjoy for their efforts.

Traveling to Devils Tower for the festive occasion required several days for some people. The towns of Sundance, Deadwood, Lead, Central, Terraville, Rapid City, Sturgis, Spearfish, Belle Fourche, Minnesela, and Beulah were all represented.

The crowd of onlookers gathered near Devils Tower on the evening of July 3, and the entertainment began. Al Storts, who was a local rancher, horse-racing enthusiast, and renowned fiddler (having played at the Chicago World's Fair) made music for the dancers, until a rain storm forced everyone to seek protection.

The rain, however, did not dampen spirits. Most people were up before sunrise and the program began soon after. Reverend Cheeseman of Spearfish and Reverend Campbell of Whitewood each delivered an oration. Next, William Engle of Centennial Prairie gave a recitation of a piece entitled "America." Then a choir of selected people on the grounds

Superintendent Newell Joyner (left) and local resident George Grenier by old stake ladder, 1932 (National Park Service file photo)

sang. Following, Reverend Cheeseman presented Rogers with a suit donated for the occasion by several ladies from Deadwood.

Since a large American flag was not readily available, a group of Sundance citizens purchased muslin at the Abe Frank store in Sundance. With the cloth, estimated at 12-by-8 feet, spread out on the saloon floor, artist Truman Fox painted the stars and stripes.

Rogers put on the suit, took the flag, and made ready for his climb. As he was leaving, two Spearfish real estate brokers, Clark and Harlow, gave Rogers a card and prospective of their business, asking him to attach it to the flagstaff.

Ripley's ascent of the Tower had not been made public, but a few people who knew about it were ready to make some money. Joyner wrote, "Quite a few large bets were made by those 'in the know' after the ascent had actually been made. They found plenty of persons who were sceptical that it could be done, and who were willing to back up their scepticism with cold cash."

Amid much cheering, Rogers made his historic ascent in approximately one hour. On the summit he secured Old Glory to the staff and then made his descent.

In the afternoon, an unexpected wind blew the flag off the Tower. Because many people present wanted a piece of it as a souvenir, the historic cloth was cut up and sold. The stars sold for 25 cents each and pieces of the stripes brought 10 cents apiece.

The crowd celebrated with much eating and dancing until the daylight hours on the morning of the fifth.

The drama of the day affected many people. *The Sundance Reform* wrote:

> (At the Bench) the Tower has a slight incline for 200 feet to the summit, and here Mr. Rogers had placed a rope which he had placed at the top of the Tower. His first climb over this 200 feet (before the rope had been placed in position) required an amount of coolness and nerve possessed by few men. Here in the air 400 feet from the ground, with only rugged pieces to assist him, he climbed and carried his rope. It was well he had the rope to assist him on the 4th, for if he had not some of the ladies no doubt would have fainted. This climb is the most wonderful ever witnessed in America and Mr. Rogers deserves all the glory he will undoubtedly receive in making it possible for man to reach the summit on one of nature's greatest wonders.

This tension also infected the two principals of the event. Apparently, something sparked a confrontation before the climb. According to Joyner, "Rogers and Ripley had a big fight the morning of the climb and Rogers not only carried the American flag, but also a 'shiner' to the top." Nevertheless, the climb was made and most estimates place their earnings for the day at $300.

Although this day was the most exciting in the life of the stake ladder, it was not the only time it was climbed. Exactly two years later, July 4, 1895, the Equality State had one of its first examples of Women's Liberation when Mrs. Rogers repeated her husband's climb. Several sources reported that Will Rogers was afraid to watch his wife's ascent, likely a feigned fear as Joyner later termed Mrs. Rogers' climb a "similar commercial celebration" and notes that they had made practice climbs together.

In the years to follow, many persons claimed to have made the trip up the Tower. The National Park Service has confirmed that about 44 of these climbs were to the summit while possibly as many as 200 other climbs were made to the top of the ladder. The last known ascent of the ladder was made in 1927 by Babe (the Human Fly) White of San Francisco. He spent two days repairing the structure and, following his climb, recommended that the lower pegs be removed to discourage other climbs. The Park Service soon after destroyed the lower 100 feet of the ladder. The upper 250 feet of the original pegs remain as a reminder to everyone of men like Rogers and Ripley and of the spirit that drove them to explore and attempt what was considered impossible.

Mrs. William Rogers, the first woman to climb the Tower, 1895 (National Park Service file photo)

Fritz Wiessner belaying Lawrence Coveny on 1937 first ascent of the Tower, using mountain climbing methods (National Park Service file photo)

A MAGNIFICENT PIECE OF CLIMBING

When Rogers and Ripley climbed the stake ladder in 1893, Devils Tower was but a rock in the wilderness. They had only to devise a way to climb it and carry out their plan. By the time alpine mountaineering techniques had progressed to the level necessary to ascend the Tower, it had been declared a national monument. This was beneficial for the rock and surrounding area but a hindrance to Fritz Wiessner and his companions in their attempt to reach the summit.

For nearly two years, a triangle of letters passed between New York, Washington, D.C., and Devils Tower. Wiessner was confident that he could make a successful ascent, but the National Park Service wanted to be sure that Wiessner's experience and equipment would be adequate to ensure safety. At last, on May 13, 1937, Fritz Wiessner received written permission for a party of three to attempt the first ascent of the Tower by mountaineering methods.

Wiessner, from New York, brought Lawrence Coveny, also of New York, and William P. House, of Pittsburgh, with him. All three were members of the American Alpine Club and had previous climbing experience. Wiessner had climbed in the Alps, Himalaya, and the Rockies of Canada, the United States, and Mexico. Coveny had much experience on smaller routes in the East, but the Tower would be his first major climb. House had experience in the Alps, Tetons, and Mexico. On their way to Devils Tower, all three stopped in the Needles area of South Dakota and climbed two spires as training for the Devils Tower climb.

Wiessner had proposed the ascent for June 28, 1937. He, House, and Coveny arrived at Devils Tower on the afternoon of June 27 and spent several hours examining the face. Wiessner had already formed an idea about where the route should be, and he showed this to the other climbers.

At 6:30 A.M. the next morning, the three set out. They were wearing "ordinary hiking clothes with wool socks and low canvas climbing shoes with heavy hempen soles, which not only gave them sure footing, but allowed them to feel the crevices with their feet. Each climber carried a thirty-five meter safety rope made of the best quality Italian hemp, which is tested to 1-1/2 tons and will stretch twenty to twenty-five feet, thus acting as a cushion to the climber in case of a fall."

The party scrambled up the talus slope to the base of a wide crack. Wiessner led up to a broken column, upon which all three could stand. "Wiessner looked over the crack when we got to the overhanging ledge, and said 'I think it goes,'" said Coveny. "I wasn't so sure, but Wiessner led us up as magnificent a piece of mountain climbing as I have ever seen."

Wiessner used a chimney technique to ascend the wide crack. Coveny later described this lead when he wrote:

> In the crack Fritz climbed at first with effort, but after some 15 feet all seemed well. A shoulder and elbow, thrust into the crack, provided the friction hold which enabled him to raise a knee. By a turn

> of the ankle sufficient pressure was maintained with heel, toe and knee to straighten his body upward and again jam shoulder and arm in the crack a few inches higher. He was now climbing rhythmically with his characteristic flawless technique. Only two regular gasps of breath which sounded like the panting of locomotive interrupted the steady cycle of upward movement. A bulge in the edge of the column forced his shoulders back but did not delay him more than a minute. At this point the intensity of preparedness on the part of Bill and myself gave way to spontaneous and complete but soft-spoken admiration. We knew that we were watching an exhibition of leading such as few climbers ever see.*

In the middle of this long crack, Wiessner stopped and hammered a piton into a smaller horizontal crack for protection. This was the only piece of protection he used, but he later declared that the piton was unnecessary and wished he had not placed it. "Every bit of the climb was made under our own power," Wiessner said. "We used no artificial means whatever."

At the end of this chimney, the climbers scrambled to the Meadows and then onto the summit, arriving at 11:18 A.M. The ascent had taken them 4 hours, 48 minutes. They spent half an hour taking photographs and gathering specimens requested by park superintendent Newell Joyner. They brought back tufts of grass, cactus in full bloom, ferns, small samples of rock taken from the peak, a Mormon cricket, and droppings from a small mammal which they assumed to be a chipmunk. Besides finding the flagpole carried up by Rogers and Ripley, they paced the measurements of the summit area and built a small cairn, placing their names inside an empty grapefruit-juice can within the cairn.

They observed that the summit of the Tower is dome-shaped rather than flat as had been previously believed. They also confirmed that the summit is oval with the north-south axis being the longest, as had been surmised by an earlier geological survey team.

Coveny, describing the descent of the party, wrote:

> We took a last view of the panorama and twenty minutes after our arrival began the descent by the same route. From the top of the steep slab, where we had unroped, we began a series of six rappels almost in a straight line to the bottom. When projecting rocks or chockstones made it possible we used rope-slings through which to pass the rope. In other places a piton was driven in and we took precautions against a fouled rope by sacrificing a carabiner on each piton.*

The climbers arrived at the bottom at 1:30 P.M., seven hours after they had begun their ascent. Joyner, carrying canteens of water, met them. "Three cans of grapefruit juice and orange juice doesn't [sic] go so very

---

*Coveny, Lawrence, "Ascent of Devils Tower," *Appalachia*, 84 (December, 1937): 481.

**Ibid.*, p. 483.

William House (left), Lawrence Coveny (center), and Fritz Wiessner (National Park Service file photo)

far," House said, "but if we had carried up all the water we wanted, we wouldn't have had any strength left to climb the Tower."

All three were proud of their accomplishment and agreed that it was a difficult climb. "I wouldn't recommend that any one except an experienced mountain climber attempt the trip we made," Wiessner said. "It is an extremely difficult climb for 200 feet, and to one who does not know mountain climbing it would be practically impossible to reach the top. A serious accident would be very likely to result. There is only one pitch on the north face of the Grand Teton in Wyoming which is as difficult in its way as this crack is on the Devils Tower."

Since the climb had not been advertised, only a small crowd had gathered to watch. One guest, however, was very eager to congratulate the successful climbers. Mrs. Alice Heppler, whose first husband was Willard Ripley who built the stake ladder with William Rogers, witnessed the Wiessner party climb and was the only person to have seen the two historic events.

Wiessner completed the day by giving his climbing shoes, a piton, a carabiner, and a short piece of the climbing rope used on the ascent to the museum at Devils Tower National Monument.

AN ISLAND IN THE SKY

The morning of October 1, 1941, was bright and clear. Newell Joyner, superintendent of Devils Tower, unfurled the American flag from the pole in front of the six-year-old park visitor center. He glanced up at the Tower and thought of the rumor he had heard the previous day about someone attempting to parachute onto the top of Devils Tower. He shook his head and walked into his office to see what Clerk Richards had planned for the day.

With the rumor still in mind, he joked with Richards. It must be just another rumor. There would be no one so foolish as to try a stunt like that, the two men assured themselves.

Had Joyner and Richards looked out the Visitor Center window, they would have seen the open parachute, supporting Charles George Hopkins, professional parachutist and holder of the world's record for the most jumps (2347), world's record for the longest delayed jump (20,800 feet), and the American record for the jump from the greatest height in the U.S. (26,400). They didn't see the historic descent. But mechanic Frank Heppler did.

Heppler burst into park headquarters at 8:15 that morning, only four minutes after Hopkins had landed. "I could not believe that he actually was there instead of at a point beyond until I saw Hopkins standing on the edge," wrote Joyner. The rumor had been true, but Joyner, when he looked up at Hopkins on the summit, had no idea what this "crazy stunt" would lead to. The landing was only the first scene of a drama that would capture the nation.

Running to the beginning of the Tower Trail, Joyner yelled up at Hopkins, asking how he planned to get down. Hopkins replied, "Why worry about that? It is no problem, is it?"

Joyner thought back on the past week. There had been more planes than usual circling the Tower and using the nearby airstrip. He hadn't paid much attention, though, because seeing the Tower from a plane answered one of the most common questions of all: "What does it look like on top?"

A man of decisive action, Joyner drove his car to that tiny airstrip. There he learned from Rapid City reporters who were already on the scene that Hopkins had reportedly jumped in hopes of winning a $50 bet. In talking with other reporters, Joyner discovered another story, the real one.

Hopkins' three parachuting records had formerly been four. His record 25 jumps in one day had been bested. He intended to get that mark back with a 30-jump day in Rapid City. As he was sponsored by the Rapid City Chamber of Commerce, all the proceeds from his record attempt would go to the benefit of the Black Hills General Hospital. The Tower jump was designed as a promotional gimmick for the benefit event the following week. No one anticipated the kind of media attention it would draw.

Hopkins, aged 30, a former R.A.F. parachute instructor, was fascinated with parachutes and their capabilities. It was this interest which impelled him "to let the people know just what a person can do with a parachute if they [sic] really know their parachutes. I had always wanted to get a 'chute so I could prove that I could hit the impossible and this is it and I could do it again."

Since the Park Service had not granted permission for the jump, and to prevent such attention-getting stunts in the future, Joyner was ordered to stop all publicity. This proved to be impossible. The man backing Hopkins, Earl Brockelsby, was efficient. At the moment Hopkins had landed, publicity had gone out by phone to New York and to 400 radio stations. Joyner knew what that meant.

As he could do nothing to prevent the publicity, Joyner probed Brockelsby about the jump. Brockelsby explained that Rapid City pilot Joe Quinn had dropped Hopkins from 2000 feet above the ground and just slightly to the south of the Tower. Quinn had made subsequent passes over the Tower and assistant Jack Gensler had dropped equipment, including a pulley, a sledge hammer, a pin made from a Ford axle sharpened on one end, and 1000 feet of half-inch manila rope. Quinn, after completing his duties, flew back to Rapid City and home.

Hopkins was then to take the steel pin, drive it into a crevice, and, using the pulley and rope, lower himself over the edge and descend to the waiting reporters. Hopkins was not a mountain climber. He knew nothing of descending ropes by rappelling but intended to use a hand-over-hand method. On paper it looked good.

However, when Gensler tossed the tightly wound rope from the plane, it hit the top of the Tower and bounced, landing on a ledge on the southeast side. Hopkins was unable to retrieve it and was stranded. Quinn could not be reached, so plans to effect a rescue had to be drawn.

Brockelsby located a Spearfish, South Dakota, pilot, Clyde Ice. Ice arrived at the Tower late in the afternoon and dropped another rope with a grappling hook. Hopkins used this rope and hook to pull up the original rope but found that it had become hopelessly tangled. Obviously, Hopkins would have to spend the night on the Tower, so Ice dropped blankets and food to him. By 6 P.M. the weather had turned cloudy and the wind prevented any further communication between Hopkins and those on the ground.

"I was up at 5:30 A.M. The morning was dreary," wrote Joyner on October 2. "Fog was rolling around the top of the Devils Tower. Some moisture fell during the night. I spent a few bad hours until around 9:00 o'clock when Hopkins first appeared. I was fearful that he had fallen victim to exposure."

The wind currents which made conversation difficult also hampered written communication. Hopkins tried writing on paper and throwing it off. One piece was seen to drop 650 feet, float back up to the top, then go up and down twice more, before being carried off out of sight. Finally Hopkins managed to drop a note attached to a rock. The note read:

> Earl or Boyd — Please get enough rope so as it will double so as you folks can lower me from the ground or help, as I feel okay but pretty week [sic] in my arms, thanks for the grub also everything else, sure am causing you lots of trouble aren't I
>
> "Devils Tower George"

By afternoon Hopkins saw the humor in his own situation. A second note commenting on goods dropped during the day read, "What, no cross-word puzzle?" Hopkins closed the same note with, "Send that blond, yet?" Before George was down, his plight was the subject of cartoons in papers and magazines across the nation.

Joyner had anticipated rescue problems in his ten years at the Tower, wondering what he would do if someone should be stranded upon the summit. By this time in 1941, only two teams of mountaineers had climbed the rock. Neither was in the area and the stake ladder, built in 1893, had been partially destroyed to prevent dangerous situations, thus making it useless in Hopkins's rescue.

With knowledge of the Tower and its vertical climbing routes so limited and with rescue by plane impossible, Joyner had no other choice but to call in expert climbers. He phoned Superintendent David Canfield of Rocky Mountain National Park and requested a rescue team. Canfield sent park ranger Ernest K. Field and Warren Gorrell, a licensed guide.

Ice returned to the Tower and made additional drops to Hopkins. Ice tried dropping an unbundled 1000-foot rope. It rolled off the northwest side and landed on the talus slope. Ice made other passes, dropping additional supplies and a tent, and Hopkins made ready to spend, as the *Rapid City Journal* wrote, "a second night on his tight little island a quarter of a mile in the Wyoming sky." Joyner noted that the evening sky provided "one of our gorgeous red sunsets which made the Devils Tower stand out in a blaze of color and which lined George Hopkins in an aura of red as he called to us good night."

In the evening, Joyner received a telegram from Jack Durrance, who had led the second ascent of Devils Tower in 1938. Joyner was pleased to hear from Durrance, because it was the consensus that his route would be the best to use for the rescue. The telegram read, "Unique first descent need any help completing it? Regards."

Field and Gorrell drove most of October 2 in a blizzard. They stopped for a few hours' sleep in Torrington, Wyoming, and finished their drive early in the morning of October 3, 1941, arriving at the Tower at 10 A.M. Joyner took them to the base to look over the route. By eleven bells they were climbing.

The storm of the previous night had coated the Tower's sides with ice. During the day, Field and Gorrell managed to attain the top of a broken column but found that they did not have the training and experience to climb the next pitch, the hardest of the route. Also, that morning Field had slipped and fallen 10 feet before the safety rope caught him. He bruised his ribs. The two returned late in the evening, admitting that they would not be able to complete the climb.

Charles George Hopkins, 1967 (National Park Service file photo)

"We both tried to ascend this pitch, frontwards, backwards, sideways, and endways — with no luck. The climb involved friction holding and wedging for a long unsecured vertical distance with no intermediate resting points," commented Field.

Field recommended that Joyner take advantage of Durrance's offer of help. At this point they realized that it might be several days before Hopkins could be rescued. Joyner called Durrance in Hanover, New Hampshire, and made arrangements for him to travel to the Tower. Joyner also sent out inquiries to a helicopter manufacturing company to see if they felt a helicopter could be used for such a purpose.

The expenses were mounting. Since the Park Service had not authorized the jump, they would not take financial responsibility. The burden fell on Hopkins's sponsors. That evening Brockelsby wrote the following note for Joyner: "This is to say that I promise to see all expenses paid in connection with the rescue of Charles George Hopkins from the top of Devils Tower saving the Government from all such obligations."

On October 4, Durrance was in transit to Devils Tower. Field and Gorrell went up to scout the route, carrying along such equipment and supplies as they could to help Durrance complete his climb as easily and quickly as possible. They hauled up an extension ladder and carried it to the top of the broken column. By 4:00 P.M. they had this ladder secured in place. This would enable Durrance to pass half of the most difficult pitch, and, as Joyner wrote, "would lessen the length of time and the amount of work required when Durrance arrived to lead the climb. The action of Field and Gorrell throughout the balance of the rescue was the greatest display of sportsmanship which I have ever witnessed. Having been hailed as the rescuers and failing to make the climb which they thought could be done without too much difficulty, they whole-heartedly bent every effort toward making the route easier and safer for Durrance."

That day Hopkins threw down a note saying, "It sure is windy up here at any spot you get. How is everybody down there? — Just eating breakfast, pulse and temperature normal, disposition has been better. Need a good bath and shave. Write me at the same address you know."

At noon, Joyner received a phone call from Acting Regional Director Paul V. Brown, saying that the Goodyear Company, following the suggestion of the Omaha *World-Herald,* was offering to send the blimp to pick Hopkins from his perch. Joyner had total confidence in Durrance being able to bring Hopkins down but told Brown that he appreciated the offer and would accept if Goodyear wanted to start the blimp on its way. "It was my feeling that we shouldn't have all our eggs in one basket; instead that we should accept any proffered help that was reasonable and without excessive expense," wrote Joyner.

In the afternoon, Durrance called the Tower from Chicago. Bad weather had grounded his plane and had changed his plans. He would arrive in Denver by Burlington Railroad. Brockelsby made arrangements for getting Durrance from Denver to Devils Tower.

Hopkins's spirits had not dampened with the weather. He sent down a note directing Brockelsby to "Phone my landlady and tell her I still want my room." To this he added the postscript, "If you get a chance, send up my morning paper."

At 9:00 in the evening, Joyner received a call from Paul Petzoldt, guide and climbing instructor in Grand Teton National Park. Petzoldt volunteered to help with the rescue. Joyner explained that Durrance was on his way, but Petzoldt "said he might come anyhow. I thanked him for the offer of his services, but did not encourage him to come," said Joyner.

On the morning of October 5, a heavy fog covered the top of Devils Tower. Joyner yelled up through the mists to Hopkins, explaining the latest developments to him. In a note, Hopkins had mentioned the rats and chipmunks on the summit. Joyner had an idea and "I asked him if he would like to have me send up a trap so that he could take some scientific specimens. I did this to provide a diversion for his mind, as well as to take steps to procure specimens that might have scientific value. He told me that he would hate to trap any of those rodents because he had been feeding them and they had become real pets. In this feeling I could sympathize and pressed the matter no further."

Just before eleven in the morning, Petzoldt arrived, along with Teton Park ranger Harold Rapp, who at 6′10″ went by the nickname of "Altitude." Joyner led them to the base where they helped Field and Gorrell, who were still working on constructing a safe route for Durrance.

By this time national press coverage had brought thousands of sight-seers and reporters. Highway patrolmen and area Boy Scouts helped keep people away from the base of the Tower and clear of the rescue team's efforts. "Our best estimate of the number of people here that day was 3500. This was in spite of the bad weather. Had the day been fair, I am certain that there would have been at least five times as many visitors."

Letters and telegrams poured into park headquarters from all over the United States offering suggestions on how to get Hopkins down. One read, "Drop Hopkins four quarts of whiskey: get him drunk. Then he'll fall off the edge. The Lord takes care of drunken people." Others made suggestions for contraptions, complete with diagrams and drawings, and still others offered to sell their ideas to the Park Service, or to complete the rescue for a price.

At 5 P.M. heavy rain and snow moved into the area. The tourists left and the climbers retired for the day. Hopkins went to bed, stranded for the fifth night. Durrance arrived at the Tower at 11:30 P.M. "We all had a feeling of anticipation in regards to the efforts of Durrance and his party on the following day," said Joyner.

Early on October 6, Hopkins "mailed" a letter to the ground crew:

> Dear Folks: Pardon my fancy stationery, but they are just out of it up here and don't know if they will stock any or not as they don't have many customers especially at this time of the year. Boy, it got so cold up here last night and so dern dreary with all that fog I would have gladly settled for a brunette or even a red head."

Hopkins had undoubtedly realized the dangerous nature of his predicament before, but expressed his thoughts by saying:

> All I worry about is someone getting hurt trying to help me, and I don't want that to happen. If I had realized how much it was putting everyone out, you can bet your bottom dollar I wouldn't have landed here, but I wanted to prove you can do damn near anything with a 'chute if you had someone that knew them — So here I am. Hope to see you all.
>
> "Devils Tower George"

Snow flurries that morning slowed the start of the rescue climb, but by 7:30 the team left with Durrance in charge. With him were Petzoldt, Rapp, Field, Gorrell, Merrill McLane (a Dartmouth student with Durrance), Chappell Cranmer, and Henry Coulter, both friends of Durrance who had joined him in Denver. When the sun appeared at eleven, Durrance had just topped the crux pitch and the climb was completed without incident. Joyner watched the entire day from the base and explained the climb in this way:

> Durrance led the climb most of the way, except for two short stretches which Petzoldt led. All eight climbers had reached the shoulder about 3:00 o'clock and at 3:15 Durrance and Petzoldt, with the former leading, reached the top of the Devils Tower and shook hands with Hopkins. Soon thereafter there were nine men on top. "House cleaning" was had and such supplies and equipment as could be brought down without hazard were bundled together and started down the side. One package lodged while the parachute and a roll containing bedding, etc., reached the bottom of the columnar portion and were retrieved the following day. The balance of the supplies were cached under rocks to relieve the unsightliness. I agree with the decision to dispose of them in this manner for time was becoming an important element at this stage in operations.

Hopkins described the climb and meeting from another point of view:

> I heard the climbers making their way slowly up the sides. I wasn't able to see them until they were within seventy-five feet of me. Durrance stopped several feet below me and waited, out of reach. He talked with me and I knew he was looking me over carefully, trying to decide whether I was going to lose my head at the thought of being rescued. When he was satisfied I was completely rational, he came over the top. That was the greatest moment! I knew for the first time I was really safe!

Joyner wrote that:

> The descent of the men was started at 4:35. Petzoldt came down first on the entire route and Durrance came down last. Hopkins had no experience in mountain climbing or rapelling [sic]; but the climbers were high in their praise of the alacrity with which he took to it, and by the time he reached the bottom he was causing them no more concern than another member of the party.

The sun set around 6 P.M. so floodlights from trucks owned by various broadcasting companies were used to light the remainder of the descent. All were safely with the waiting Joyner and Brockelsby at 8:20.

At the base, Joyner observed that:

> Hopkins' condition was remarkable, I believe, in view of the hazards which he could not escape. The wind blew continuously; he was unprotected from the weather except such protection as he could get on the lee side of a small boulder; his blankets were sopping wet; he had gotten little rest or sleep; and he had had very little drinking water. It is my belief that a normal person would have been affected by the thought of being marooned, but Hopkins' nature is such as to make him take things as they come. I am convinced that he would have attempted any means of getting himself off of the top of the Devils Tower which we would have permitted or ordered even though he realized that to do so might be the equivalent of committing suicide, rather than to have caused harm to come to anyone else.

Opposite: Hopkins's rescue party around model of the Tower (Black Hills Studios photo)

THE RAPID CITY DAILY JOURNAL

"The Newspaper of Western South Dakota"

HOPKINS RESCUE ATTEMPT STARTS

Says Reds Beat

HIS RESCUE BELIEVED NEAR

At Least 25 Persons Have Climbed To Top Of Devil's Tower

PHOTOS OF HOPKINS' RESCUE

THREE YEARS OLDER THAN THE STATE OF WYOMING

Sheridan Press

ALPINISTS SEEK TO RESCUE HOPKINS

Win World Series Crown

Climbers Promise Rescue Today; Press Correspondent Sights Stranded Man From Airplane

THE VOICE OF THE ROCKY MOUNTAIN EMPIRE

THE DENVER POST

Bundles of Food

THE SUNDANCE TIMES

Rescued After Six Days On Devil's Tower

GEORGE HOPKINS RESCUED FROM DEVIL'S TOWER MONDAY

HOME

Chicago Daily Tribune

THE WORLD'S GREATEST NEWSPAPER

CHUTIST ON WAY DOWN PEAK!

ies; Beat Dodgers, 3-1

Linked by Rope to 8 Rescuers on Rocky Wall

SHOWING HOW LUCKY WE ARE IN AMERICA

Hopkins's rescue made headlines across the country (Black Hills Studios photo)

This little meeting of nine people on the summit of Devils Tower had its price in many ways. It had taken six days to organize, during which Clyde Ice had made 73 drops from his airplane to support Hopkins. The rescue team had collectively traveled 16,000 miles, and expenses of approximately $2000 were incurred.

Early the next morning, October 7, the crowds had dispersed. The reporters packed up their equipment and returned to write their stories. The climbers left for their journeys to school, work, and families. Hopkins and Joyner drove to Sundance for a comprehensive interview with NBC before Hopkins continued on to Rapid City to prepare for his world-record attempt. Fate was against Hopkins that October. Not only did he have to spend six days on the summit of Devils Tower, but he was forced to end his attempt to regain his record after the thirteenth jump because of bruises and a sore ankle.

Joyner returned to Devils Tower and his office. There he sat down and wrote, "One Charles George Hopkins landed on the top of Devils Tower by parachute from a plane at 8:11 A.M. October 1, 1941. Such an occurrence, with its many ramifications, surely calls for a special report which is presented herewith." He proceeded to complete a 20-page single-spaced, typed report to the director of the U.S. Department of the Interior, quite possibly the longest single document in the files of Devils Tower National Monument. Surely Joyner appreciated the cold, quiet months of the winter of 1941–42.

PART THREE

Climbing Information

GENERAL CLIMBING INFORMATION

Federal law requires that anyone climbing above the talus slope must register with a park ranger before climbing and upon returning. A sign-out/sign-in sheet is at the Visitor Center during the summer months and at the Administration Building the remainder of the year.

Climbers need to plan on adequate time (four to nine hours for most routes) in order to avoid being caught by nightfall. Plenty of water should be carried for the party as well as rain gear in the summer months.

Weather should always be considered as an element in climbing at Devils Tower. Occasionally, violent thundershowers, lightning, hail, or high winds may be encountered. Afternoon showers are common and even a short shower can make the rock slick because lichen growing on the rock absorbs the water. This can instantly add one or two grades to the climbing difficulty.

Most locals consider April through June and September through early November to be the best times to climb. July and August are often very hot and unpleasant for long climbs. Mild winters in some years have found climbers making ascents in all months, although January and February are usually too cold.

The rock at Devils Tower, a volcanic neck, is phonolite porphory. It is solid and could be compared in hardness to Teton or Yosemite granite. Although some loose rock may be found in the upper sections, holds are generally secure and rarely break off. Care should be taken when working on column tops where loose rocks and debris accumulate. Rockfall from above also poses a danger at any time.

Some of the approaches to the routes are high and exposed and climbers may wish to use ropes as needed. Climbers are responsible for their own safety and must remember that no rescue team exists at Devils Tower National Monument.

Opposite: National Park Service steel rappel anchor (Steve Gardiner photo)

Climbing Devils Tower entails unavoidable risks that every climber assumes and must be aware of and respect. The fact that a route is described in this book is not a representation that it will be safe for you. Routes vary greatly in difficulty and in the amount and kind of experience and preparation needed to enjoy them safely. Some routes may have changed or deteriorated since this book was written. Also, of course, climbing conditions can change even from day to day, owing to weather and other factors. A route that is safe in good weather or for a highly conditioned, properly equipped climber, may be completely unsafe for someone else or under adverse weather conditions.

You can minimize your risks by being knowledgeable, prepared, and alert. There is not space in this book for a general discussion on climbing techniques and safety, but there are a number of good books and public courses on the subject, and you should take advantage of them to increase your knowledge. Just as important, you should always be aware of your own limitations and conditions existing when and where you are climbing. If conditions are dangerous, or if you are not prepared to deal with them safely, change your plans! It is better to have wasted a few hours or days than to be the subject of a bad fall or rescue. These warnings are not intended to keep you from climbing the Tower. Many people climb the Tower safely every year. However, one element of the beauty, freedom, and excitement of climbing is the presence of risks that do not confront us at home. When you climb Devils Tower you assume those risks. They can be met safely, but only if you exercise your own independent judgment and common sense.

No climbing school or guide service is run at the Tower. Because of the difficulty of even the easiest climbs, all climbers should have experience in climbing and the leader must be resourceful for a successful and enjoyable climb.

In rating each climb,we have used the free rating in place of any aid rating that may have previously existed. The difficulty ratings of climbs at Devils Tower are usually a consensus and seem to be fairly consistent. For example, one route rated 5.9 should be close in difficulty to another 5.9 route. In some cases, minor disagreement over a particular rating was present among local climbers and we have, in these few cases, chosen the higher rating in the interest of safety. However, many people who visit Devils Tower from other climbing areas have commented that the routes are underrated, stating, for instance, that the Durrance Crack, rated 5.6, would be 5.7 in many other areas. We recommend that climbers new to the Tower start conservatively to find out if the ratings are the same as those at their local crags.

Many climbers have come to Devils Tower to work on their aid-climbing techniques, and several good routes exist. In order to preserve the nature of the routes, please do not drive pitons into aid routes that have been climbed free. Climbers who are interested will find descriptions of all aid routes available at the Monument. Also, sixteen-by-twenty-inch black-and-white photographs showing all aid- and free-climbing routes are available. Contact a ranger to see either of these items.

A healthy poison ivy crop grows in cracks and on several of the larger ledges, notably beneath The Window and on the Northeast and Northwest Buttress approaches. Avoid dragging ropes and other equipment through these areas. Rattlesnakes may be more commonly found on the talus slopes near the base of the Tower than elsewhere in the Monument.

In constructing this guidebook we have followed a few guidelines which may help the reader. The routes are numbered from left to right on the photographs in a counterclockwise circle around the Tower. The identifying number for each route has generally been placed to the left of the route or directly on the route line where feasible. We have tried to show one or more routes overlapping at the edges of each photograph to aid in the location of climbs.

Because of the crumbly nature of the rock near the summit, the original finishes to a handful of routes may be unknown or a route may have more than one finish. Where possible we have given the original finish or the most popular finish.

In this book we have used the terms route, climb, and pitch loosely with no direct bearing on the length of the piece of climbing.

In describing the routes, we have followed, wherever possible, the written accounts provided by climbers and on file at the Monument. We have diverged from those accounts only as required by changing conditions, the need for clarity, or conventions of grammar, spelling, and usage. Readers who wish to consult the original climbers' accounts may do so at the Monument.

Anyone with additional information or corrections regarding routes in this book is asked to submit written comments to this address: Superintendent, Devils Tower National Monument, Devils Tower, WY 82714.

RATINGS OF ROUTES

Ratings of climbs are an average of what the difficulty is believed to be. External factors such as weather can change that rating sharply. The rock at the Tower is very slick when wet; immediately after a rainstorm a route will be harder to climb. The heat of summer can also be a factor, as the rock is often too hot to touch and the dehydration caused by heat can decrease a climber's endurance and make the route seem harder.

The Roman numeral grading represents the approximate time element involved in a climb. The divisions of this are:

Grade I — a short climb of less than two hours.
Grade II — a slightly longer climb of two to four hours.
Grade III — a climb of four to eight hours.
Grade IV — a long climb requiring eight to twelve hours.

Grade V — a two-day climb requiring an overnight.
Grade VI — a multi-day climb.

The free routes at Devils Tower are rated by the Yosemite Decimal System. The numbers of that system represent the degree of difficulty presented by the terrain. The six classes are as follows:

Class 1 — walking on level ground.
Class 2 — off-trail walking with some uphill and light scrambling.
Class 3 — scrambling that includes the use of the hands for support and balance.
Class 4 — scrambling that demands a rope for protection against exposure, but intermediate points of protection are not used.
Class 5 — technical rock climbing using ropes and intermediate protection.
Class 6 — direct aid climbing in which the leader uses the pieces of protection for support and advancement.

Climbers familiar with the Yosemite Decimal System will have little trouble interpreting the ratings for whole climbs or individual pitches. Others, who come from areas using other rating systems, may find the following conversion scale helpful in interpreting a rating.

UIAA	DECIMAL	NCCS	BRITISH
I	1	F1	Easy
II	2 & 3	F2	Moderate
III−	4	F3	Moderately Difficult
III	5.0		
III+	5.1	F4	Difficult
IV−	5.2		Very Difficult
IV	5.3	F5	Severe
IV+	5.4		
V−	5.5		
V	5.6	F6	Very Severe
V+	5.7	F7	Hard
VI−	5.8	F8	
VI	5.9	F9	
VI+	5.10	F10	
VII−	5.11		
VII	5.12		

Climbers must be reminded that ratings are subjective. No one has climbed all the routes at Devils Tower and even if one person had, his judgment would still be subjective. At best, ratings are an approximation of difficulty, but they are influenced by many factors. For example, the routes at Devils Tower are crack climbs. A climber who has trained in other crack-climbing areas might find a given route very easy and straightforward, while a climber from a face-climbing region might find the same line an impossible task.

Each route is given a rating by the first ascent party at the time of the first ascent. The Yosemite Decimal System has not been a static one. When it was designed, 5.9 was supposed to be the hardest climb humanly possible. Eventually there were climbs rated 5.9 that were much harder than others rated 5.9, and 5.10 and other classifications were created. Thus, routes that were originally rated 5.9 (because there was no alternative) may be 5.10 or harder by today's standards. Some care in choosing routes that fit into this category would be wise.

As the Yosemite Decimal System developed, finer gradations than the numerical values developed and merit mention here. While the limit of technical rock remained at 5.9, many climbers added a plus/minus rating. In this book there are examples of routes rated 5.8+ or 5.9–. This should be interpreted to mean that a route overall deserved a given rating but certain factors colored the tone of that rating. A 5.8+ route should be seen as a difficult 5.8 route that may have a move or two that might be interpreted as 5.9.

As the system developed through 5.10, 5.11, 5.12, and, now, 5.13, the plus/minus system seemed to fade out and another method emerged. Climbers, wishing to distinguish between various 5.10 climbs, attached an additional a, b, c, or d rating following the 5.10. For example, a 5.10a climb would be the easiest climb that could still be rated 5.10. A 5.10d climb would be the hardest rated 5.10 and might, by a different climber, receive a 5.11 rating.

Direct aid climbing routes are rated on a scale of A1 to A5 with the easiest climb being an A1 and the hardest being an A5, although the most difficult rating at Devils Tower at this time is an A4, The Window. Most aid routes at Devils Tower are a combination of aid climbing and free climbing and thus will have two ratings (for example, 5.7-A2) in addition to the Roman numeral grades.

As with records and standards in any sport, the rating system for technical climbing will likely continue to grow and expand, reflecting the quality of the participants in the sport and the ever-increasing difficulty of the routes they complete.

CLIMBING STATISTICS

Devils Tower is unique in that all climbing is done in one area and the Park Service has been able to record historical data with a high degree of accuracy. Monument records contain information about every ascent since Weissner in 1937. A quick look at such information is interesting and shows the growth of climbing as a sport and of the popularity of Devils Tower as a climber's destination. All the numbers below reflect successful summit climbs by year.

YEAR	YEARLY PARTIES	YEARLY CLIMBERS	ALL-TIME PARTIES	ALL-TIME CLIMBERS
1937	1	3	1	3
1938	1	2	2	5
1939	0	0	2	5
1940	0	0	2	5
1941	2	10	4	15
1942	0	0	4	15
1943	0	0	4	15
1944	0	0	4	15
1945	0	0	4	15
1946	1	2	5	17
1947	1	2	6	19
1948	2	18	8	37
1949	3	20	11	57
1950	1	2	12	59
1951	5	13	17	72
1952	7	19	24	91
1953	8	27	32	118
1954	12	42	44	160
1955	5	17	49	177
1956	53	158	102	335
1957	11	46	113	381
1958	42	143	155	524
1959	32	119	187	643
1960	42	104	229	747
1961	50	123	279	870
1962	55	128	334	998
1963	36	92	370	1090
1964	75	187	445	1277
1965	48	119	493	1396
1966	33	100	526	1496
1967	51	134	577	1630
1968	53	136	630	1766
1969	71	184	701	1950
1970	82	216	783	2166
1971	103	297	886	2463
1972	138	357	1024	2820
1973	121	312	1145	3132
1974	164	424	1309	3556
1975	183	494	1492	4050
1976	308	774	1800	4824
1977	445	1098	2245	5922
1978	657	1638	2902	7560
1979	805	1969	3707	9529
1980	701	1754	4408	11,283
1981	667	1624	5075	12,907
1982	428	1277	5503	14,184
1983	617	1621	6120	15,805
1984	629	1266	6749	17,071
1985	648	1591	7397	18,662

Only in 1974 did the Park Service start keeping records of unsuccessful attempts.

YEAR	UNSUCCESSFUL CLIMBERS	ALL-TIME UNSUCCESSFUL CLIMBERS
1974	88	88
1975	117	205
1976	168	373
1977	183	556
1978	532	1088
1979	659	1747
1980	1053	2800
1981	1700	4500
1982	1753	6253
1983	1995	8248
1984	1870	10,118
1985	2625	12,743

APPROACHES TO THE ROUTES

All approaches leave from the Visitor Center parking lot.

Durrance Approach — Take the right fork of the Tower Trail heading east to the end of the first boulder field by the pine trees on your left. Climb the talus angling to the left of the obvious slab to the base of the Tower below the McCarthy West Face route. From there scramble up and right to a large broken column which leads to the Southwest Shoulder. Traverse this shoulder to the right staying near the outer edge all the way around. At the end of the shoulder scramble up to the base of the Leaning Column.

South Face Approach — Turn right at the fork in the Tower Trail and go east, circling around the Tower until you are directly below the Wiessner route in the main indentation (Bowling Alley) on the South Face. At this point you will be just short of the trail junction to the Binoculars. Scramble up the slope to the base of the Meadows Rappel.

The Ramp — At the top of the South Face Approach, look slightly up and right and see a long ledge leading east. Follow this ledge for 100 feet where, just after a large flake, there is an obvious corner junction. Climbing up and left of this corner leads to Bon Homme and the Stake Ladder area. To continue up The Ramp, drop eight feet and pass the corner. Just beyond the corner the angle of The Ramp steepens for 120 feet until you climb over a large flake. From there drop down and around the corner to the ledge beneath Soler, TAD, and El Cracko Diablo. The narrow ledge continues descending around one more corner where it becomes the large shelf beneath Tower Classic and The Window.

East Buttress Approach — Take the right fork of the Tower Trail and continue past The Window to a large fallen column beside the trail. Go 150 feet past the column to a faint trail on the left where you will be directly beneath the East Buttress. Leave the trail and climb up the right side of the shallow gully to the base of the buttress. Traverse up and right on a climbers' trail to a constriction (Hourglass) between the East and Northeast buttresses. From this constriction traverse up and left to the top of the East Buttress by one of several routes. Poison ivy thrives above the constriction on this route.

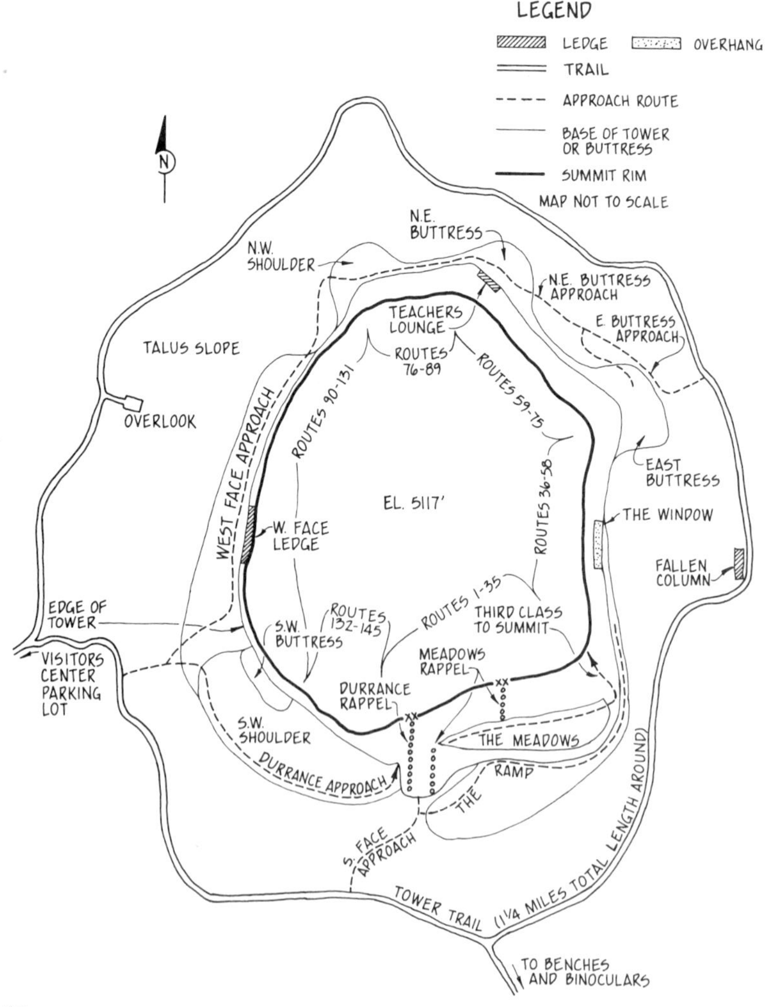

Northeast Buttress Approach — Follow the East Buttress Approach to the Hourglass and traverse up and right until you reach the top of the Northeast Buttress below the Teacher's Lounge ledge. The buttress may be followed west to the Northwest Buttress beneath the Northwest Corner route.

West Face Approach — Leave the Tower Trail the same as for the Durrance Approach. At the top of the talus slope where it meets the trees, traverse up and left to the sloping shoulder which may be followed all the way to the northwest corner of the Tower.

STANDARD MEADOWS FINISH

Once you reach the Meadows you will be able to pick up a well-worn trail on the upper edge of the Meadows that runs east and west. Follow the trail to the right (east) to a point where it narrows and enters a small notch formed by the cliff face and a boulder. Downclimb five feet through the notch, traverse right a few feet and then climb up over large chockstones. An obvious chimney leads up 140 feet to a face just below the summit. Climb up and right across this face to where you can easily walk up to the summit. A short walk leads to the actual summit cairn where a register is located in a metal container.

Though the scramble is not difficult, exposure is encountered, and it is recommended that you fourth class this section as a fall here could be very serious or fatal.

RAPPEL ROUTES

Summit Rappels

There are three standard routes of descent from the summit of Devils Tower. All three routes are marked by cairns on the south side of the summit dome.

While you are looking south, the cairn on your right (southwest) marks a set of rappel bolts which may be reached by downclimbing 15 feet to a ledge. From the bolts, look down and note that you can throw your rope well to the left or down right. By throwing your ropes (need two) left (as you face out) it is possible to rappel down to the west end of the Meadows beside the Jump Traverse and above the Meadows Rappel bolts. By throwing your ropes (need two) straight down or right, you will land at the bolts on the ledge above Pitch 5 (Chockstone) of the Durrance route (separated from the Meadows by the Jump Traverse). It is possible to rappel from here down to the ground on the Durrance route with a single rope, but this is discouraged because there is almost always a party climbing the Durrance and much loose rock can be dropped on climbers below.

A second method of leaving the summit is from the middle cairn. Rappel bolts are found several feet below this cairn and a rappel from here (with two ropes) will place you in the middle of the Meadows.

The third method of descent is marked by the left or easternmost cairn (as you look from the summit). This is the top of the Standard

Meadows rappel route (Dick Guilmette photo)

Meadows Finish, and many climbers prefer to downclimb to the Meadows (third or fourth class, exposed).

Meadows Rappel

From the Meadows, two rappel routes have become standard. The first, built by the Park Service (two eye bolts drilled eight inches into solid rock and cabled together) is found at the west end of the Meadows on a ledge some 25 feet below the spot where a fallen column forms a tunnel. If you climb the Durrance route, stop on the top of Pitch 5 (Chockstone). Looking across the Jump Traverse and slightly down and to your right, you will see the bolts for descent. This route requires two ropes as the rappels average 140 feet.

Throw your ropes directly out over the nose of a large ledge below these bolts and be sure to place your rope on a flat section about two feet wide as you walk down the nose. Over 50 percent of all rescues come about because rappel ropes slide into the left or right crack and the knot gets stuck there when the ropes are being pulled down and the climbers are unable or unwilling to climb to the top to free the rope. With the ropes on the flat of the nose this will not happen. The next bolts are directly below you on the shorter of two obvious columns.

Rappel straight down the column and the next bolts will be found on a ledge just above a large tree and about 30 feet below where the column turns into the blocky base of the Tower.

One more rappel leads to level ground, and the South Face Approach may be used in reverse to return to the Tower Trail and Visitor Center and parking lot.

Bon Homme Rappel

The other rappel route from the Meadows, placed by local climbers, is on the Bon Homme route. Four anchors exist so a two-pitch rappel on two ropes or a four-pitch rappel on one rope may be used.

To locate the top of this rappel, follow the trail in the Meadows to the west to a point where it climbs steeply up to the column forming the tunnel. Instead of climbing up, stay level and approach a large boulder. Downclimb to find the bolts.

Rappel straight off the ledge and note a column top below you. For a single rope, stop at the bolts at the column top. For a double rope, rappel down the right side of this column (facing in) and land on a boxed-in column top below. Pull the rope down on the left (west) side or the knot often jams in the right crack.

As you rappel off this ledge, leave your ropes as far to the left (west) as possible. For a single rope, stop at the bolts halfway down the face and just above a pointed flake affectionately known as the Rope Eater (hanging rappel). Rappel to the bottom and pull your rope from a tree at the left (west) end of the ledge.

Downclimb third class for 50 feet to meet The Ramp. Follow it down and west to the base of the Meadows Rappel, and again reverse the South Face Approach to reach the Tower Trail.

Note: Though these rappel routes are in constant use, climbers are responsible for their own safety and should examine, but not strike, any rappel anchors they decide to use. If a climber does not like an anchor, he should place his own protection and not use anything he is not fully satisfied with.

POPULAR AND RECOMMENDED CLIMBS

RATING	ROUTE, CLIMB, OR PITCH
5.6	Durrance
5.7	TAD
5.8	Bon Homme, Horning Variation
	El Cracko Diablo
5.9	Soler
	Assembly Line
	Walt Bailey Memorial
5.10a	New Wave
	Tulgey Wood
5.10b	Belle Fourche Buttress
	Burning Daylight
	Jerry's Kids
5.10c	Hollywood and Vine
	One-Way Sunset
	Everlasting
5.10d	Casper College
	El Matador
5.11a	McCarthy North Face
	Carol's Crack
	Mr. Clean
5.11b	Direct Southwest
	No Holds For Bonzo
5.11c	McCarthy West Face
	McCarthy West Face — Hong Variation
5.11d	Digital Extraction
	Direct Southeast
	Avalon
5.12a	Bloodguard
	Brokedown Palace
5.12b	Let Me Go Wild
	Object Cathexis
5.12c	Surfer Girl
	Hollow Men
A1	Zephyr
A2	Misty Morning Melody
	Butterfingers
A3	Blade City
	Centennial
A4	The Window

First ascent of Potatoes Alien (Route 102), 1985, with Mateo Pee Pee leading and Barney Fisher on belay (Dick Guilmette photo)

South Face

ROUTE DESCRIPTIONS

South Face

1. DURRANCE II, 5.6

FIRST ASCENT: September 8, 1938, by Jack Durrance and Harrison Butterworth. **APPROACH:** Take the Durrance Approach.

PITCH 1: Leaning Column. Climb the face and obvious crack until you can get behind the left side of the column where it breaks. From here work up behind the column or stem up the side (80 feet, 5.6). There are fixed pins in this section. **PITCH 2:** Durrance Crack. Jam the right crack while stemming over to the left crack most of the time and moving over into the right crack near the top (72 feet, 5.6). There are fixed pins in this lead and nuts can be secured in the left crack. There is a good chockstone partway up the right side. **PITCH 3:** Cussing Crack. Climb up the outside of the crack a few feet and you will find a good spot for two #4 wired stoppers on the left. Then finish the chimney to a good narrow ledge that can be traversed around to the right. Climb up a few feet to the bolts via a good crack (30 feet, 5.5). **PITCH 4:** Flake Crack. Climb the corner crack and face to the top of the pitch onto a large ledge (40 feet, 5.5). You can take the Conn Traverse from here by a long step onto the face of the right column, down a crack 12 feet onto a platform and up the other side to the Meadows, and finish on the Standard Meadows Finish. **PITCH 5:** Chockstone Crack. Chimney up the large crack, passing a chockstone and overhang near the top (40 feet, 5.4). **PITCH 6:** Jump Traverse. Move out to the right on the downsloping slab beneath the overhang, swing around the corner, then step across to the other side; an old piton around the corner and a small, horizontal finger crack facilitate the crossing (15 feet, 5.6 if you hold onto the piton and 5.8 if free climbed). Jumping is not recommended. **FINISH:** Standard Meadows Finish.

SUGGESTED EQUIPMENT: Medium to large Hexentrics, Stoppers or Friends, and runners.

2. PIGEON ENGLISH II, 5.9

FIRST ASCENT: April 14, 1984, by Paul Piana and Bill Hatcher. **APPROACH:** Complete the Durrance Approach to the base of the Leaning Column. The route starts at the break of the column and is two cracks left of the belay bolts at the top of it.

PITCH 1: Same as Durrance (Route 1), Pitch 1 (80 feet, 5.6). **PITCH 2:** Step down and left into the Pigeon English crack. Hand jamming followed by fist and then some off-width leads to the extreme end of the crack, which is the hardest part of the route. (A thin flake continues up and right.) At this point traverse left at the base of what appears to be a huge, loose block. When a chimney (Manifest Destiny, Route 145) is reached, follow it to large ledges where a belay may be set (160 feet, 5.9–). **FINISH:** Three options exist. 1. Traverse right to the Meadows and take the Standard Meadows Finish. 2. Rappel off. 3. Climb the crack above you to the summit.

SUGGESTED EQUIPMENT: Take medium to large pieces (from 3/4 to 5 inches) and a few runners.

NOTE: Use care on the traverse and notify the rangers if the block above it moves or appears to be especially dangerous. Problems with rope drag may occur if protection is placed beyond the apex of the Pigeon English crack. The original climbers placed no protection in the Manifest Destiny portion of Pitch 2 and found no moves harder than 5.5 but reported it as a long runout.

3. PERSISTENCE II, 5.9

FIRST ASCENT: May 17, 1980, by Steve Gardiner and Frank Sanders. **APPROACH:** Take the Durrance Approach to just past the Leaning Column. Scramble up and right on blocks to the base of the Durrance Column. The route goes up its right side.

PITCH 1: Gotcha. Climb this off-width crack using jamming and face holds to the right. Belay from the NPS bolts on top of the Durrance Column, Route 1 (150 feet, 5.8). **PITCH 2:** Hang in there. Cross the column top and take a long, traversing step to the left to reach the crack that leads up to the obvious roof 25 feet above. Climb this off-width crack through the roof and a smaller one just beyond. Continue to a large ledge where this route meets Manifest Destiny, Route 145 (145 feet, 5.9). **FINISH:** Same as Manifest Destiny finish (150 feet, 5.6).

SUGGESTED EQUIPMENT: Standard rack of Stoppers and Hexentrics plus extra large Hexentrics and some tube chocks for protecting the off width. Large Friends would help.

4. BAILEY DIRECT II, 5.5
(One pitch variation of Durrance, Route 1)

FIRST ASCENT: February 2, 1958, by Walt Bailey, Raymond Jacquot, Jim Kothel, Richard Williams, and Kenneth Johnson. **APPROACH:** Same as Durrance up to the top of Pitch 5 (Chockstone Crack).

PITCH 6: At the top of Chockstone Crack (Jump Traverse bolts), climb up and left on moderate fifth-class climbing to the top. Belay at the Durrance Rappel bolts just below the summit (150 feet, 5.5). A variation of this is to go left one crack from the Jump Traverse bolts and climb straight up until you merge with the Bailey Direct route halfway up. Continue to summit. **FINISH:** Scramble and walk to the summit.

SUGGESTED EQUIPMENT: Medium to large Hexentrics, Stoppers or Friends, and runners.

5. SUNDANCE II, 5.7
(Starts on Wiessner and ends on Durrance)

FIRST ASCENT: August 17, 1958, by Bob Kamps, Dave Rearick, and Verena Frymann. **APPROACH:** Take the Durrance Approach, then traverse right to the base of Wiessner (Route 7) to the bottom Meadows rappel bolts.

PITCH 1: Same as Wiessner, Pitch 1. Climb up right and then left to the base of the two broken columns that stairstep up to the right. Climb the left side of the lower column to the top of that column. Then climb the left-hand crack, which is Sundance, onto a column top with a bush growing just below its top. Belay from the column top (120 feet, 5.6). **PITCH 2:** Climb the jam crack that runs up the face directly above you until you reach the ledge that marks the top of the Flake Crack on the Durrance Route (Route 1) and belay from the eyebolts there (155 feet, 5.7). (You can make this in two pitches by traversing to the top of Cussing Crack on the Durrance Route, about 95 feet, and belaying there before continuing on.) **FINISH:** You have several options here. The recommended routes are the Conn Traverse, Durrance (Jump Traverse), or Durrance/Bailey Direct (Route 4) to the summit.

SUGGESTED EQUIPMENT: A few small pieces with the rest medium to large Hexentrics, Stoppers, and tubes. Large Friends are helpful.

6. MATEO TEPEE II, 5.7, A3

FIRST ASCENT: July 2, 1984, by Steve Gardiner and Joe Sears. **APPROACH:** Take the Durrance Approach to the base of the Leaning Column and continue on ledges down, right, and up to the Meadows Rappel bolts.

PITCH 1: Traverse right and up on a sloping ledge until it meets with another similar ledge leading to the left. Follow this ledge up and around the Wiessner Column (Route 7) and belay from a large horn (50 feet, 5.4). **PITCH 2:** Stem the wide crack behind the column by using a narrow crack on the left. Climb up the first column, onto a large ledge, and continue up a similar stemming crack system to the top of the Wiessner Column (70 feet, 5.6). Pitches 1 and 2 are sometimes done in one pitch now. **PITCH 3:** Mateo Tepee. Climb the shallow crack on the left of Pseudo-Wiessner (Route 8) on aid. Use a Lost Arrow in a horizontal crack to reach the main crack and climb on thin aid using RURPs, tied-off knifeblades, and sky hooks for 25 feet. At this point the crack flares. Another horizontal crack on the left face provides the first solid protection on the pitch. Above here the crack is filled with loose rock, dirt, and bushes. It may be climbed by using nuts and larger pitons to a large bush where free climbing takes one to the Conn Traverse and up to the Meadows. Belay from the upper rappel bolts (150 feet, 5.7, A3). **FINISH:** Standard Meadows Finish.

SUGGESTED EQUIPMENT: Standard free rack for the first two pitches and for Pitch 3 bring a collection of RURPs, sky hooks, knifeblades, bugaboos, and tie-off loops.

7. WIESSNER II, 5.7

FIRST ASCENT: June 28, 1937, by Fritz Wiessner, William House, and Lawrence Coveny. **APPROACH:** Take the Durrance Approach to the base of the Leaning Column. Then traverse right and down to the first set of rappel bolts which are the bottom bolts of the Durrance rappel.

PITCH 1: Climb directly up to the base of the two broken columns that stairstep up to the right. These are located just below and to the left of Wiessner Crack. Climb the left side of the columns and belay from the top of the upper column. An easier way, commonly used today, is to climb up to the right past the first bolts to a second set at the base of the Meadows Rappel. Then climb up and traverse back to the left to the base of the two broken columns and climb to the belay bolts (120 feet, 5.6). **PITCH 2:** Wiessner Crack. From the top of the highest of the two columns climb down three or four feet to the right and make the long stretch across to the right-hand crack that is off width and jam your way to the top of the Wiessner Column (65 feet, 5.7). The lower portion is hard to protect. A long runner can be used to tie off a large chockstone three-quarters of the way up the crack. **PITCH 3:** Climb straight up above the Wiessner Column until you reach the large platform at the lower left-hand corner of the Meadows; it is part of the Conn Traverse. Climb the right corner crack to a large ledge and belay from the Meadows Rappel bolts (55 feet, 5.4). **FINISH:** Standard Meadows Finish.

SUGGESTED EQUIPMENT: #5 to #8-1/2 Stoppers, #6 to #9 Hexentrics, tube chocks, and runners.

8. PSEUDO-WIESSNER II, 5.8

FIRST ASCENT: August 10, 1954, by Ray Northcutt and Harvey T. Carter. **APPROACH:** Take the Durrance Approach to the base of the Leaning Column. Then traverse right and down to the last rappel bolts for the Durrance Rappel route and start from there.

PITCH 1: Climb up right, and then back left, from the eyebolts to the base of the two broken columns that stairstep up to the right. These are located just below and to the left of Wiessner Crack. Climb to, and belay from, the top of the higher of these two columns (120 feet, 5.7). **PITCH 2:** Climb the crack that runs directly up from the column you are belaying from, passing two currant bushes, until you reach a good belay ledge (90 feet, 5.8). This is a hand/fist crack with some off width. **PITCH 3:** Climb straight up until you reach the west end of the Meadows by the Jump Traverse. Many people now climb up the right crack past the Meadows rappel bolts (35 feet, 4). **FINISH:** Standard Meadows Finish.

SUGGESTED EQUIPMENT: Medium to large Hexentrics, tube chocks, extra #4 Friends, extra #10 to #11 Hexentrics, and runners.

NOTE: The original climbers went directly up after Pitch 3. This is seldom, if ever, done today.

9. EXTENDED WIESSNER I, 5.8

FIRST ASCENT: June 25, 1977, by unknown climbers. **APPROACH:** Same as Wiessner (Route 7) to the lower Durrance Rappel bolts. Belay there.

PITCH 1: Climb up and right to the lower Meadows Rappel bolts. From here proceed up a few more feet until you can traverse back left and work up to the base of Wiessner Crack itself. You are now boxed in between two broken off columns on your left and the Wiessner Column (Route 7) on your right. Most climbers utilize both the left and right cracks by stemming back and forth between them while concentrating on the left crack. Climb up any way you wish to the topmost broken column on your left and belay here (120 feet, 5.8). This is the top of Wiessner, Pitch 1. **FINISH:** You can rappel off from here or continue up on Wiessner or Pseudo-Wiessner (Route 8).

SUGGESTED EQUIPMENT: Same as Wiessner.

M&CWTC #3 and #4 (Old Army Aid Routes) II, Aid

FIRST ASCENT #3: July 12, 1956, by Cecil M. Ouellette and Charles Kness. **FIRST ASCENT #4:** July 14, 1956, by Marcus Russi and John Callahan.

South Face

EXPLANATION: These routes are/were located in the Durrance–Sundance area and the Path of Dissent area. Very little is known about the exact route locations; therefore they are not described or located on photos. The M&CWTC stands for the "Mountain and Cold Weather Training Command," an army group that climbed at the Tower.

NOTE: The unnumbered routes in this guidebook are included for historical accuracy and completeness. Evidence of each climb exists, and each route is included in topographical order, but a number is not assigned since not enough detail is available to include the route on a photograph or in a written description.

10. DEVILS DELIGHT—DIRECT I, 5.7

FIRST ASCENT: September 8, 1974, by Dennis Horning, Judd Jennerjahn, and Rob Wheeler. **APPROACH:** Same as Devils Delight (Route 11). This route follows the right side of the Wiessner Column (Route 7).

PITCH 1: From the bolts, climb up and into the jam crack that starts on the right side of the bottom of the Wiessner Column. Instead of climbing up 30 feet and traversing right, stay in the initial crack all the way up to the NPS Meadows Rappel bolts (135 feet, 5.7). This chimney takes large pieces. **FINISH:** Rappel off or continue up Devils Delight and Wiessner to your left or take the harder Path of Dissent (Route 12) which is the crack on your right.

SUGGESTED EQUIPMENT: 6- to 7-inch tubes and equipment for Devils Delight and Wiessner.

NOTE: This route is not often done because of the need for tubes, etc. (off width).

11. DEVILS DELIGHT (M&CWTC #1) II, 5.8+

FIRST ASCENT: July 9, 1956, by Cecil Ouellette and Charles Kness (II, Aid). **FIRST FREE ASCENT:** July 2, 1962, by John Evans and Dennis Becker. **APPROACH:** Take the Durrance Approach to the base of the Leaning Column, then traverse down to the right past the lowest Durrance Rappel bolts and up to the bottom Meadows Rappel bolts. This route essentially follows the aid route M&CWTC #1, though the exact location of some portions of the aid route is disputed.

PITCH 1: From the bolts, climb up and into the jam crack that starts on the right side of the bottom of the Wiessner Column (Route 7). Climb about 30 feet until it becomes possible to traverse right to the next crack. Climb 15 to 20 feet up this crack and traverse right to the next crack. Climb this crack 20 to 25 feet and traverse right one crack. Now climb this short, widening jam crack past a currant bush in the crack to a ledge formed by two column tops. Traverse left across three columns and climb 25 feet up to the top of the column, where you will find the middle set of Meadows Rappel bolts (125 feet, 5.8+). **PITCH 2:** Climb to the top of the Wiessner Column on your left. From here to the Meadows is Pitch 3 of the Wiessner route. Climb the cracks that run straight up from the top of the Wiessner Column to a small platform at the west end of the Meadows (100 feet, 5.5). **FINISH:** Standard Meadows Finish.

SUGGESTED EQUIPMENT: #5 to #8-1/2 Stoppers, #6 to #10 Hexentrics, tube chocks, and runners.

12. PATH OF DISSENT II, 5.9

FIRST ASCENT: July 30, 1979, by Mark Smedley, Jim Black, and Rich Jaskiewiez. **APPROACH:** Use the Durrance Approach, then traverse right past the Durrance Rappel bolts to the bottom Meadows Rappel bolts and belay here.

PITCH 1: Traverse right up ramps until you are one crack left of Sunfighter (Route 13). Proceed up this crack and belay on the column top to your left (140 feet, 5.9). **PITCH 2:** Climb the dirty crack that leads up the left side of the Meadows Rappel overhanging block at the top of the pitch (155 feet, 5.8). There is loose rock on this pitch. **FINISH:** Standard Meadows Finish.

SUGGESTED EQUIPMENT: #1 to #8 Hexentrics, #3 to #12 Stoppers, 4-inch piece, and extra medium to large Hexentrics.

M&CWTC #5 (Old Army Aid Route) II, Aid

FIRST ASCENT: July 16, 1956 (exact army climbers unknown).

EXPLANATION: Monument records show a drawing of this route and date but the sketch is not accurate enough to be certain of the route's location. It looks like they first went up one crack left of the Wiessner Column to the column top that ends the first pitch of Wiessner. From here it shows a pendulum (one or more) across several columns to the right. This includes traversing right one crack past what is shown as "MTC 1" (probably M&CWTC #1), then climbing up to a belay above. From here the sketch shows them climbing up a short distance and then traversing right one column and climbing up to the Meadows from here. This last portion may be the present Path of Dissent route.

NOTE: The unnumbered routes in this guidebook are included for historical accuracy and completeness. Evidence of each climb exists, and each route is included in topographical order, but a number is not assigned since not enough detail is available to include the route on a photograph or in a written description.

13. SUNFIGHTER II, 5.8+

FIRST ASCENT: August 31, 1975, by Dennis Horning and Jim Slichter. **APPROACH:** Same as Wiessner (Route 7). Belay from the upper set of the lowest rappel bolts (lowest Meadows Rappel bolts). This crack is one crack left of The Best Crack in Minnesota (Route 14) and five cracks right of Wiessner Crack.

PITCH 1: Traverse to the right from the bolts to a large ledge at the start of the crack. The crux of the pitch is to reach a ledge left of the crack a short distance up. This can be liebacked. The hanging belay is about even with the rappel bolts, about eight feet below the last bush in the crack (150 feet, 5.8+). **PITCH 2:** Chimney up the crack to the Meadows Rappel bolts (135 feet, 5.6). **FINISH:** Standard Meadows Finish.

SUGGESTED EQUIPMENT: #1 to #8 Hexentrics, #2 to #12 Stoppers, five 2- to 5-inch pieces, and slings to tie off chockstone.

14. THE BEST CRACK IN MINNESOTA I, 5.9

FIRST ASCENT: July 20, 1984, by Paul Piana, Bob Cowan, Todd Skinner, and Beth Wald. **APPROACH:** Take the Durrance Approach to the base of the Leaning Column, then traverse right past Wiessner (Route 7) until you are at the start of Sunfighter (Route 13).

PITCH 1: Begin with the initial moves of Sunfighter and, a short distance above the ledge, move right into what certainly would be The Best Crack in Minnesota, if the poor souls at Taylor Falls were lucky enough to have it. This is a pitch of good hand jamming right to the top of the crack. From here, step right to an anchor (around the arête) and contemplate the interesting problem below (100 feet, 5.9). **FINISH:** Rappel from the anchor.

SUGGESTED EQUIPMENT: #2 and #3 Friends and medium Stoppers.

15. JOURNEY TO IXTLAN II, 5.10b

FIRST ASCENT: June 9, 1976, by Dennis Horning and Perry Ohlsen. **APPROACH:** Take the Durrance Approach, then traverse right until you reach the crack well past the rappel bolts. This route lies between Sunfighter (Route 13) and Danse Macabre (Route 16). It is marked by two large bushes, with two smaller bushes on each side of the larger ones.

PITCH 1: Climb to the first small bush doing very hard stemming. Two fixed pins protect these moves. The crux (flared crack) is getting from the higher smaller bush to the lower larger bush. A #5-1/2 Stopper is a good quick-draw piece for the crux. Continue climbing to a good belay ledge on your right (140 feet, 5.10b). **PITCH 2:** Continue climbing the now wide crack to the top of the column, and finish at the Meadows Rappel bolts (130 feet, 5.7). At the top you can also scramble up right to the Meadows. **FINISH:** Standard Meadows Finish.

SUGGESTED EQUIPMENT: #1 to #8 Hexentrics, #3 to #12 Stoppers, 5-inch tube, and *extra* #6 to #12 Stoppers and large Hexentrics.

16. DANSE MACABRE II, 5.10d

FIRST ASCENT: August 19, 1964, by Royal Robbins and Peter Robinson. **APPROACH:** Same as Wiessner (Route 7). Traverse right to the route about 10 cracks right of the Meadows Rappel. Start on top of a flake or pinnacle, between Journey to Ixtlan (Route 15) and Bittersweet (Route 17).

PITCH 1: Traverse to the right crack on a difficult move. Jam the crack with fingers and hands until you are about 30 feet below a roof overhead. Traverse left to a crack above a bush and follow that crack to a ledge on your left. Belay here (160 feet, 5.10d). **PITCH 2:** Climb the large crack through the roof to a belay ledge on your left at the Meadows (80 feet, 5.9). **FINISH:** Standard Meadows Finish.

SUGGESTED EQUIPMENT: #1 to #8 Hexentrics, #3 to #12 Stoppers, and four or five extra large Hexentrics and 4-inch pieces.

NOTE: The original party did not finish on the Standard Meadows Finish but climbed straight up and slightly left to the summit from the end of Pitch 2. This is not used anymore.

17. BITTERSWEET II, 5.10c

FIRST ASCENT: September 25, 1977, by Dennis Horning and Frank Sanders. **APPROACH:** Follow the South Face Approach, then traverse right on The Ramp to the first corner. Climb up as for Bon Homme (Route 24), but then turn left and work your way up and back to the start of the route. This route lies two cracks to the right of Danse Macabre (Route 16) and two cracks to the left of Delta I (Route 19).

PITCH 1: Climb the crack almost to its end (145 feet, 5.10c). There are two difficult sections. One is encountered 20 feet off the ground and is poorly protected by nuts. The second hard section is some 30 feet higher just above a horizontal ledge that affords good protection. There are several fixed pins in the first hard section. Set up a hanging belay. **PITCH 2:** Do a delicate traverse left to the next crack. Continue up the increasingly easy crack until you reach the Meadows for a belay (130 feet, 5.6). **FINISH:** Standard Meadows Finish.

SUGGESTED EQUIPMENT: A full set each of Stoppers and Hexentrics; runners for pitons and chockstones. Also extra Stoppers and #9 and #10 Hexentrics.

18. MORCHELLA ESCULENTA II, 5.11c

FIRST ASCENT: June 1, 1979, by Larry Wydra and Tom Ptacek (II, 5.7, A3). **FIRST FREE ASCENT:** September 6, 1980, by Dennis Horning and Mark Smedley. **APPROACH:** Follow the South Face Approach and traverse right on The Ramp until you come to the first corner. From here climb straight up under the Bon Homme (Route 24) rappel to the large tree on the left. The route is the crack left of this tree. It is one crack right of Bittersweet (Route 17) and one crack left of Delta I (Route 19).

PITCH 1: Climb up this left-curving, overhanging finger crack through a roof to the belay bolts on your right (150 feet, 5.11c). **PITCH 2:** Follow the wide crack above you through some bushes and past a column top on your right to the Meadows (150 feet, 5.7). **FINISH:** Standard Meadows Finish.

SUGGESTED EQUIPMENT: Take #1 to #8 Hexentrics, #3 to #12 Stoppers, and extra small to medium Stoppers, Hexentrics, and Friends.

NOTE: The last few feet of Pitch 2 are on Delta I.

19. DELTA I II, 5.9−

FIRST ASCENT: October 31, 1964, by Bob Schlichting and Bill Heatley (II, 5.8, A2). **FIRST FREE ASCENT:** September 15, 1976, by Dennis Horning and Frank Sanders. **APPROACH:** Take the South Face Approach and traverse right on The Ramp until you are below the large roof. Climb up to the route. This route lies three cracks left of the largest roof on the South Face and one crack left of Waterfall (Route 20). Belay from the highest juniper tree.

PITCH 1: Stem and climb the Waterfall crack to the top of the bushes. Then move into the Delta I crack and continue to a good flake on the left. Place some good chocks. The next section, 35 feet, offers excellent hand and toe jamming with little opportunity for further protection placement. Belay at the bolts (125 feet, 5.9–). **PITCH 2:** Climb and stem a Durrance-like crack to the top of the column on your right (60 feet, 5.7). **PITCH 3:** (variation of aid route Delta I): Traverse right to the next crack and climb up for about 40 feet, then cross a face to your left on friction and continue up the crack to the Meadows. The original free-route third pitch was done this way. You can also climb up the 5.5 crack directly above (120 feet, 5.5). **FINISH:** Standard Meadows Finish.

SUGGESTED EQUIPMENT: A full set of Hexentrics and larger Stoppers. Also several 3- to 4-inch pieces.

NOTE: The old aid route Delta I finish is favored and can be done in one pitch. From the bolts at the top of Pitch 1, climb and stem to the column top on your right and then continue up the crack above you where you can belay from a column top on your left (155 feet, 5.5). Take the scramble up the left crack to the Meadows.

20. WATERFALL II, 5.9–

FIRST ASCENT: May 31, 1976, by Dennis Horning, Skip Fossen, and Mark Santangelo. **APPROACH:** Same as Delta I (Route 19). Belay from the juniper tree. This crack lies one crack right of Delta I and one crack left of B. O. Plenty (Route 21) on the South Face.

PITCH 1: Climb the crack through the roof, past a large (loose?) flake, to a height equal to that of the roof on B. O. Plenty (140 feet, 5.9–). This belay stance is much improved by the use of a seat. **PITCH 2:** Continue up the crack on your left to the top of the column on your left (70 feet, 5.8). The upper portion is a difficult off-width crack. **PITCH 3:** Climb to the Meadows via the crack that bisects the belay column (100 feet, 5.5). Note that pitches 2 and 3 can be combined by belaying on a left column top just short of the Meadows and then scrambling up the left crack from there. **FINISH:** Standard Meadows Finish.

SUGGESTED EQUIPMENT: #4 to #8-1/2 Stoppers, #5 to #11 Hexentrics, and three or more 4-inch pieces.

21. B. O. PLENTY II, 5.9–

FIRST ASCENT: August 18, 1970, by Charles Bare and Jim Olson (III, A2). **FIRST FREE ASCENT:** September 16, 1976, by Frank Sanders and Dennis Horning. **APPROACH:** Take the South Face Approach, then traverse right on The Ramp to the first corner and up to the base of the Bon Homme Rappel (Route 24). You should now be one crack right of the large juniper tree.

PITCH 1: Belay from some large flakes at the base of the crack. These flakes are about the same height as the highest juniper tree. About 15 feet up a few thin moves gets one to easier climbing. Finish the last 12 feet below the roof with a gentle but committing lieback. Belay from a small ledge to the left of the roof (130 feet, 5.9–). **PITCH 2:** Stem and jam the crack on the left to the top of the left column. From here continue straight up an easy chimney and belay from the large ledge on your left (155 feet, 5.8). **FINISH:** Standard Meadows Finish.

SUGGESTED EQUIPMENT: #1 to #8 Hexentrics, #3 to #12 Stoppers, extra large Hexentrics, and some 4-inch pieces.

19
24
23
24
30
32
33
25
27
20
24
33
35
20
32
19
23
27
28
29
24
26
30
31
34
18
19
22
21

South Face

22. SEAMSTRESS II, 5.12c

FIRST ASCENT: March ?, 1982, by Chris Engle and Dave Johnson (II, A2). **FIRST FREE ASCENT:** June ?, 1982, by Steve Hong and Karin Budding. **APPROACH:** Same as Bon Homme (Route 24). This route is two cracks left of the start of Bon Homme and one crack right of B. O. Plenty (Route 21).

PITCH 1: Belay high and climb up this long, hard pitch using fingerlocks, stemming, and face holds. It is 5.11 near the first two bolts and the crux is climbing from the last bolt to the roof. The roof is an easy 5.10. This pitch ends at the Bon Homme ledge bolts (155 feet, 5.12c). **FINISH:** Rappel off, or continue up to the Meadows on Bon Homme or Second Thought (Route 25) and then take the Standard Meadows Finish to the summit.

SUGGESTED EQUIPMENT: #1 and #2 Friends and 25 small wired nuts with a few quick draws. If you go to the top, take equipment for Bon Homme or Second Thought.

NOTE: The protection on the crux is difficult to place but OK once you have it. The bolts are drilled out a little too far so watch for rope drag.

23. BON HOMME, HORNING VARIATION II, 5.8

FIRST ASCENT: November 5, 1972, by Dennis Horning and Howard Hauck. **APPROACH:** Same as Bon Homme (Route 24). Belay on a high ledge above the dead tree.

PITCH 1: Climb the Bon Homme crack past the chockstone. Traverse left across the column below the small roofs (crux) on the face and above a small bush in the crack to the left. Continue on up the double crack to a good ledge (155 feet, 5.8). **PITCH 2:** Climb the left crack; same as Pitch 2 of Bon Homme (150 feet, 5.5). **FINISH:** Standard Meadows Finish.

SUGGESTED EQUIPMENT: Medium to large Hexentrics and Stoppers, plus small wired Stoppers for the traverse. Friends help.

24. BON HOMME II, 5.9

FIRST ASCENT: August 20, 1958, by Bob Kamps and Donald Yestness. **APPROACH:** Take the South Face Approach to the base of the Meadows Rappel. Traverse The Ramp to the right 100 feet to a corner junction. Climb third class up to the base of the columns. This route starts four cracks left of the old Stake Ladder (see Route 29). Belay on a high ledge above the dead tree.

PITCH 1: Climb about 100 feet in this large crack, six to eight inches wide, and traverse left around the column below a small roof on the face of the column. Climb the double crack in the left-facing dihedral to a great belay ledge on a column top (155 feet, 5.9). A more popular variation of this pitch is the Horning Variation (Route 23). **PITCH 2:** Climb the left crack to the column top on your left. Continue straight up from here past a bush to the Meadows and belay at the bolts (150 feet, 5.7). Some climbers belay at the left column top and then climb to the Meadows. **FINISH:** Standard Meadows Finish.

SUGGESTED EQUIPMENT: A few small wired Stoppers, tubes, and medium to large Hexentrics and Stoppers.

25. SECOND THOUGHT II, 5.7
(last pitch variation of Bon Homme, Route 24)

FIRST ASCENT: September 28, 1977, by Dennis Horning and Howard Hauck. **APPROACH:** Same as Bon Homme.

PITCH 1: Same as Bon Homme, Horning Variation (Route 23) to the bolts at the column top. **PITCH 2:** Second Thought. Climb the sustained right hand crack to the Meadows (140 feet, 5.7). **FINISH:** Standard Meadows Finish.

SUGGESTED EQUIPMENT: Same as Bon Homme.

26. UNCLE REMUS DIRTY VEGETABLE GARDEN II, 5.4, A2

FIRST ASCENT: September 14, 1972, by Mike Brown and Frank Sanders. **APPROACH:** Same as Bon Homme (Route 24). Start at the first crack to the right of Bon Homme.

PITCH 1: Nail up this dirty crack using bugaboos, two-inch angles, Lost Arrows, and small tied-off angles. Continue up on small bongs as the crack widens through small trees, and set up a hanging belay in the crack on your right (160 feet, A2). **PITCH 2:** Continue up this widening crack to the top of a very large, very loose flake then step across, as the crack flares, to a narrower crack (standard angles) on your left. Use three or four solid aid pins, then go free; traversing up and right and finish on top of a column (35 feet, 5.4, A2). **FINISH:** Standard Meadows Finish.

SUGGESTED EQUIPMENT: Three bugaboos, ten or more Lost Arrows, six baby angles, five standard and five 7/8-inch angles, four 1-1/2-inch angles, and five bongs up to 4 inches. Large Chouinard chocks (#7 to #10) would go well in top crack. A belay seat helps.

NOTE: Pitch 2 follows Double Indemnity (Route 27).

27. DOUBLE INDEMNITY II, 5.11a

FIRST ASCENT: May 24, 1980, by Steve Hong, Karen Budding, and Mark Smedley. **APPROACH:** Use the South Face Approach and The Ramp. At the first corner junction of The Ramp, climb up to the start of the route. The route is two cracks left of the old Stake Ladder (Route 29) and two cracks right of Bon Homme (Route 24).

PITCH 1: Climb this crack about 90 feet stemming left one crack much of the time. Traverse right one crack on a large hold when the crack becomes too small to continue, but do not cross too early. Follow this crack (Speedway) for 15 feet and hang the belay on a small ledge with double bolts (105 feet, 5.11a). **PITCH 2:** Speedway. Follow this flaring hand crack for 35 feet. Traverse left one crack from a large hold on the left. Follow this crack to the Meadows (135 feet, 5.10d). **FINISH:** Standard Meadows Finish.

SUGGESTED EQUIPMENT: Many small and medium Stoppers, #1 and #2 Friends, one small RP for crux, and numerous slings.

NOTE: On a scale from one to three, Steve Hong rates this a one-star route.

28. ENGLISH BEAT II, 5.12b

FIRST ASCENT: May 14, 1978, by Terry Rypkema and Steve Gardiner as the aid route Speedway (II, A3). **FIRST FREE ASCENT:** July 22, 1984, by Todd Skinner, Paul Piana, Bob Cowan, Frank Hill, and Kevin Lindorff with belaying/ encouragement by Beth Wald. **APPROACH:** Take the South Face Approach and traverse right on The Ramp until you are just short of the corner. Climb up and right to the route from here. This route lies one crack left of the old Stake Ladder (see Route 29).

PITCH 1: Move into the crack from blocks between Double Indemnity (Route 27) and the target climb by utilizing a diagonal fracture that enables one to reach the leaning fingerlocks that only suggest the difficulty of the crux above. The crux is a series of wild, out-of-control, lieback moves to a flared crack that is comparatively easy but still 5.11. This is a test-piece climb with intellectual moves, desperate protection for the crux, and a need for an up-tempo rock-and-roll approach to solving the moves. It is desperate until it joins Double Indemnity. Belay at the bolts on your right (110 feet, 5.12b). **PITCH 2:** This is Pitch 2 of Double Indemnity. The crux is a short distance above the belay bolts. Shortly above the crux and before the crack ends, traverse left one crack. Climb up this crack until you are nearly level with the top of the crack on your right. Traverse up left and back up to the right at a bush. Belay at the bolts on your right just above a bush (135 feet, 5.10d). **FINISH:** Scramble to the Meadows and take the Standard Meadows Finish to the summit.

SUGGESTED EQUIPMENT: Many small and medium Stoppers, a set of Hexentrics, RPs, # 1 and # 2 Friends, and runners.

NOTE: English Beat is one pitch and you can rappel off from the bolts if you do not want to go to the summit or Meadows.

29. CARPENTER'S CAPER II, 5.7, A2

FIRST ASCENT: July 10, 1972, by Terry Rypkema, Roger Holtorf, and Bruce Bright.

NOTE: Use of this route is prohibited because of its proximity to the Stake Ladder which must not be disturbed, damaged, or removed. Carpenter's Caper is two pitches of mixed free and aid climbing and was established by seasonal rangers in the process of making approved repairs to the Stake Ladder.

30. THE POWER THAT PRESERVES II, 5.12a

FIRST ASCENT: April 2, 1978, by Terry Rypkema and Frank Sanders as Afternoon Delight (II, A2). **FIRST FREE ASCENT:** July 12, 1983, by Todd Skinner and Moana Roberts, who jumarred and belayed. **APPROACH:** Same as Bon Homme (Route 24). The route is the first crack left of Direct Southeast (Route 31) and two cracks right of the Stake Ladder (see Route 29). This route follows the Afternoon Delight aid crack.

PITCH 1: This depressingly thin fingertips crack has stemming and fair protection. The crux is approximately 90 feet up and sustained. Set up a hanging belay from the bolts at the horizontal crack (155 feet, 5.12a). **PITCH 2:** Continue up the enjoyable finger and hand crack to the Meadows (70 feet, 5.10). **FINISH:** Standard Meadows Finish.

SUGGESTED EQUIPMENT: Pitch 1 — many RPs, #2 to #3 Stoppers and Sliders, and #1 Friends. Pitch 2 — small Stoppers and #2 and #2-1/2 Friends for the top section.

NOTE: There is a loose flake about two and one-half feet square right at the top that must be avoided. This is one of *the best* 5.12a routes on the Tower. A three-star classic according to Todd Skinner.

31. DIRECT SOUTHEAST II, 5.11d

FIRST ASCENT: May 1, 1965, by Peter Oslund and John Horn (II, 5.5, A2). **FIRST FREE ASCENT:** August 24, 1978, by Steve Hong, Mark Smedley, and Karin Budding. **APPROACH:** Take the South Face Approach to the base of the Meadows Rappel, then traverse right on The Ramp until you can third class up to the base of the climb. The route is three cracks right of the old Stake Ladder (see Route 29).

PITCH 1: Belay at the base of the thin crack. This is a variable finger crack with occasional natural finger pockets. Climb up on continuous, thin moves that get progressively harder until you reach a stance belay on fixed pins that are located in a horizontal crack to the left (160 feet, 5.11d). **PITCH 2:** Continue up this crack until you reach the Meadows (50 feet, 5.7). **FINISH:** Standard Meadows Finish.

SUGGESTED EQUIPMENT: Three sets of RPs, many #1 to #8 Stoppers, one #1 Friend, and two #2 Friends.

NOTE: Steve Hong rates this climb a three-star classic.

32. WALT BAILEY MEMORIAL II, 5.9

FIRST ASCENT: July 26, 1959, by Gary Cole, Raymond Jacquot, and Charles Blackmon (II, 5.8, A2). **FIRST FREE ASCENT:** May 27, 1974, by Jeff Overton and Scott Woodruff. **APPROACH:** Take the South Face Approach to the base of the Meadows Rappel. Traverse right on The Ramp until you are just below some large blocks at the southeast corner of the Tower. The route starts on top of these blocks and is four cracks right of the old Stake Ladder (Route 29). Climb to the start of the route, left of Hollywood and Vine (Route 35). This is third- or fourth-class climbing (very exposed).

PITCH 1: Climb left and immediately traverse up and right to the top of the flake. Climb the left finger and hand crack to the Meadows (165+ feet, 5.9). The belayer may have to climb a few feet so the leader can reach the Meadows belay ledge. **FINISH:** Standard Meadows Finish.

SUGGESTED EQUIPMENT: #1 to #9 Hexentrics, #2 to #12 Stoppers, and extra #4 to #12 Stoppers.

NOTE: Many climbers consider this route one of the finest 5.9 pitches on the Tower.

33. PHILLIP'S RETREAT I, 5.9+

FIRST ASCENT: July 22, 1978, by Dennis Horning with a belay by Phillip Chandler. **APPROACH:** Take the South Face Approach to the base of the

Meadows Rappel. Traverse right on The Ramp until you are just below some large blocks at the southeast corner of the Tower. The route starts on top of these blocks and is one crack right of Walt Bailey Memorial (Route 32) and one crack left of The D.O.M. (Dirty Old Man), Route 34. Third or fourth class up to the start of the route. This is very exposed and many use a rope.

PITCH 1: This route follows the first 20 feet of Walt Bailey Memorial and then continues up the right finger crack from the top of the flake. Follow the finger crack and then move right a short way into a leaning dihedral for a short distance before moving back left also for a short distance. Now traverse up to the right to the next crack (a left-leaning dihedral), climb this a few feet, and set up a belay (160 feet, 5.9+). **PITCH 2:** Climb the same crack to the Meadows (30 feet, 5.4). **FINISH:** Standard Meadows Finish.

SUGGESTED EQUIPMENT: Small to medium Hexentrics, small to large Stoppers, and extra medium to large Stoppers.

NOTE: Pitch 2 is on The D.O.M., an old aid route.

34. THE D.O.M. II, A2 or A3

FIRST ASCENT: September 4, 1967, by Ron Howe, Terry O'Donnel, and Evans Winner. **APPROACH:** Same as Walt Bailey Memorial (Route 32).

EXPLANATION: Park records indicate the first and second ascents of The D.O.M. but no route description or photo location has been found. Tradition has been that the route is one left of Hollywood and Vine (Route 35), and we are marking this crack for government records.

PITCHES 1 AND 2: Nothing is definitely known about this crack except that two pitches will get you to the Meadows. **FINISH:** Standard Meadows Finish.

SUGGESTED EQUIPMENT: No suggestion given by first-ascent climbers.

NOTE: D.O.M. stands for Dirty Old Man.

35. HOLLYWOOD AND VINE II, 5.10c

FIRST ASCENT: May 8, 1960, by Gary Cole and Raymond Jacquot (III, 5.5, A1). **FIRST FREE ASCENT:** May 26, 1974, by Jeff Overton and Scott Woodruff. **APPROACH:** Take the South Face Approach. Traverse right on The Ramp toward the southeast corner of the Tower. The route starts on the right side of the highest broken column on the southeast corner. There is quite a bit of poison ivy on this section of the shoulder, but it can easily be avoided.

PITCH 1: Climb the chimney on the right side of the broken column and belay from the bolts on top of the column (75 feet, 5.5). **PITCH 2:** Using fingerlocks and stemming, climb up the old aid crack in the center of the shallow dihedral to a ledge at the top of the crack (160 feet, 5.10c). The crux, fingertip liebacking on pin scars, is halfway up this pitch. **PITCH 3:** A short pitch of easy free climbing brings one to the Meadows (40 feet, 5.4). **FINISH:** Standard Meadows Finish.

SUGGESTED EQUIPMENT: #1 Hexentrics, lots of #1 to #12 Stoppers, and runners.

NOTE: A 165-foot rope is necessary for Pitch 2 in order to stretch this lead to a ledge at the top of the crack.

East Face

36. SOLER II, 5.9–

FIRST ASCENT: August 30, 1951, by Tony Soler, Art Lembeck, Herb Conn, Ray Moore, and Chris Scordus. This was the first tension climb on Devils Tower. **FIRST FREE ASCENT:** May 2, 1959, by Layton Kor and Raymond Jacquot. **APPROACH:** Take the South Face Approach to the base of the Meadows Rappel. Traverse The Ramp to the right until you just turn the southeast corner below Hollywood and Vine (Route 35) to the next crack, which is Soler. The crack is in a right-facing dihedral and is considered by many to be one of the better climbs.

PITCH 1: From a high but small belay ledge begin the climb and continue up the crack. A comfortable hanging belay can be set up above the chockstones at bolts (150 feet, 5.8+). **PITCH 2:** Continue up the crack to its finish at the Meadows (110 feet, 5.9–). **FINISH:** Standard Meadows Finish.

SUGGESTED EQUIPMENT: Full rack of Hexentrics through #8 and Stoppers mid-range through large, with extra #8 to #12 Stoppers and #4 to #7 Hexentrics.

NOTE: There is no crux, as such — simply two pitches of well-protected and continuous hand jams and liebacks. The original aid party did not finish in the same crack but worked its way out onto the left face about 30 feet below the Meadows for an easy finish. This is not used much now as climbers prefer the straight line.

37. TODTMOOS II, 5.9–

FIRST ASCENT: May 1, 1976, by Dennis Horning and Jim Slichter. **APPROACH:** Same as TAD (Route 38). The climb lies in the crack between Soler (Route 36) and TAD.

PITCH 1: Climb up to, through, and above the bushes to a hanging belay at a horizontal crack on the right (125 feet, 5.9–). The difficult move of this pitch is just below the first bush. **PITCH 2:** Continue up the crack to a belay at the Meadows (145 feet, 5.8+). There are some 5.8+ moves in this pitch. The upper parts of the pitch are hard to protect because of dirt and moss in the crack. **FINISH:** Standard Meadows Finish.

SUGGESTED EQUIPMENT: #1 to #8 Hexentrics, #3 to #12 Stoppers, and extra small Stoppers; a belay seat helps.

NOTE: Dirt and bush climb; infrequently done.

38. TAD (M&CWTC #2) II, 5.7

FIRST ASCENT: July 10, 1956, by Dave Gallagher and Jack Morehead. **FIRST FREE ASCENT:** July 3, 1973, by Dan Burgette and Charles Bare. **APPROACH:** Take the South Face Approach to the base of the Meadows Rappel. Traverse The Ramp to the right until you turn the southeast corner. The crack you want is two cracks right of Soler (Route 36), which is in the right-facing dihedral. Originally this was done in three pitches.

East Face

PITCH 1: Climb the crack to a small slanting ledge, just below where the crack begins to narrow, and set up a semi-hanging belay (120 feet, 5.7). **PITCH 2:** Climb straight up on hand and fist jams to the Meadows (150 feet, 5.7). The crack flares for a short distance just below the Meadows. **FINISH:** Standard Meadows Finish.

SUGGESTED EQUIPMENT: Friends, assorted small nuts, medium to large Stoppers, and Hexentrics with extra large pieces.

NOTE: A letter in park files by Jack Morehead shows that the name of this route comes from the exclusive Playful TAD Climbing Club which is composed of only four people, two of whom are the first-ascent climbers listed above. Others have thought it represented Third Armored Division or Tactical Army Demonstration Team.

39. EL CRACKO DIABLO II, 5.8

FIRST ASCENT: October 21, 1973, by Rod Johnson and Pat Padden. **APPROACH:** Take the South Face Approach and traverse The Ramp all the way around until you are one crack right of TAD (Route 38) and one crack left of Exit-US (Route 41).

PITCH 1: Climb a short face just left of the crack for a few feet, then step into the jam crack. Climb this hand crack and off width until you reach a narrow ledge system that leads to the hanging belay bolts well out on the right face (120 feet, 5.7). **PITCH 2:** Climb this crack on foot and hand jams while utilizing small face holds on the right face. The crux is about 40 feet up at a bulge above a fixed bong where some off width is encountered. Belay at the bolts on the right block (150 feet, 5.8). **FINISH:** Standard Meadows Finish.

SUGGESTED EQUIPMENT: #4 to #11 Hexentrics, large Stoppers, and extra medium to large pieces. Large Friends are helpful.

NOTE: There is a problem with loose rock and dirt at the upper belay.

40. EXTENSION II, 5.10d

FIRST ASCENT: July 21, 1985, by Dennis Horning and Jim Schlinkmann. **APPROACH:** Same as El Cracko Diablo (Route 39). The route lies one crack right of Pitch 2 of El Cracko. The route follows the Exit-US (Route 41) crack above the bolts. (The Exit-US route traverses right above the bolts, whereas Extension follows the crack straight up.)

PITCH 1: Same as El Cracko Diablo, Pitch 1. **PITCH 2:** From the belay bolts at the end of Pitch 1 of El Cracko, follow the right crack to bolts on the Meadows ledge (140 feet, 5.10d). The climbing is very delicate, with lots of face moves and weird crack climbing. The crux is encountered about halfway up the pitch, where the crack thins out. Protection isn't abundant, but there are some creative placements in the shallow crack. Three bolts help protect the second half of the pitch. **FINISH:** Standard Meadows Finish.

SUGGESTED EQUIPMENT: Full set of Stoppers, RPs, Friends to #2, small to medium Hexentrics; sliders and quick draws very helpful.

41. EXIT-US II, 5.9

FIRST ASCENT: July 6, 1968, by Dave Ingalls and Roy Kligfield (II, 5.5, A2). **FIRST FREE ASCENT:** September 27, 1976, by Frank Sanders and Dennis Horning. **APPROACH:** Exactly the same as Cave (Route 42), including the bottom belay. This route is one crack left of Cave and starts one crack right of El Cracko Diablo (Route 39) on the East Face. We recommend that you fourth class up to the belay ledge.

PITCH 1: Take the left crack from the belay ledge. Climb the crack up the corner and through a dihedral, surmounting a bulge. Continue using crack and face holds until you come to a hanging belay position at the bolts on the left face (140 feet, 5.9). **PITCH 2:** From the belay, traverse right up sloping ramps to the next crack, which is Cave. Climb the second pitch of Cave to the Meadows and belay there (155 feet, 5.9). **FINISH:** Standard Meadows Finish.

SUGGESTED EQUIPMENT: #3 to #9 Hexentrics, many #1 to #12 Stoppers.

NOTE: Some climbers think that Exit-US is derived from "Exodus." Park records do not give any information on this. The route is very dirty and not climbed much.

42. CAVE II, 5.9

FIRST ASCENT: August 26, 1965, by Pete Oslund and Dave Ingalls (II, 5.5, A2). **FIRST FREE ASCENT:** September 20, 1976, by Dennis Horning and Frank Sanders. **APPROACH:** Take the South Face Approach, then traverse right on The Ramp until you are just past TAD (Route 38). Look up and see the Cave hole. Climb exposed fourth or fifth class up to a high belay ledge on the face between Exit-US (Route 41) and Cave. The Cave route is three cracks right of TAD.

PITCH 1: Belay high up on a good ledge to the left of the dihedral below the roof. Climb up the dihedral onto a friction slab and then turn the roof on the left. Rope snag can be a problem here. Continue about 25 feet past the roof to a horizontal crack that makes for a good standing belay (150 feet, 5.9). There are some fixed pins in the lower dihedral. This pitch affords poor small Stopper protection. **PITCH 2:** Continue up the hand-jam crack to its end at the base of the Meadows finish (145 feet, 5.8). Ample protection is afforded by Stoppers. **FINISH:** Standard Meadows Finish.

SUGGESTED EQUIPMENT: A set of Hexentrics through #9, #2 to #8-1/2 Stoppers and RPs. Extra #9 Hexentrics and small and large Stoppers.

43. LAST COWGIRL CAMP II, 5.11b

FIRST ASCENT: October 6, 1968, by Pete Oslund and John Chuta as Second Cave (II, 5.7, A2). **FIRST FREE ASCENT:** August 27, 1979, by Dennis Horning and Jay Smith. **APPROACH:** Take the South Face Approach and Ramp until you are below Cave (Route 42). This route starts five cracks right of the prominent dihedral (Soler, Route 36) on the southeast corner of the Tower.

PITCH 1: Belay from an adequate ledge at the start of Exit-US (Route 41). From here traverse right to the next crack, which is Cave. Ascend the dihedral, turning the roof of the cave on the right, and continue to a small belay stance 25 feet above the roof on your left (140 feet, 5.9). **PITCH 2:** Continue up the right-facing dihedral stemming, liebacking, and crack climbing to the base of the Meadows (140 feet, 5.11b). **FINISH:** Standard Meadows Finish.

SUGGESTED EQUIPMENT: #1 to #12 Stoppers, #3 to #9 Hexentrics, many #1 to #2 Friends, and extra #1 to #12 Stoppers.

NOTE: This free climb is believed to be on the old aid route Second Cave. Some think the aid route was climbed one crack right of Last Cowgirl Camp, or in the crack where Troglodytes Trauma (Route 44) starts. Piton placements and pin scars were found in the Last Cowgirl Camp crack, but none have been reported in the crack to the right.

44. TROGLODYTES TRAUMA II, 5.11c

FIRST ASCENT: April 22, 1971, by Ian Wade, Barbara Euser, and Walter Fricke (II, A3). **FIRST FREE ASCENT:** June 14, 1979, by Jim Beyer and Dennis Horning. **APPROACH:** Follow the South Face Approach and The Ramp until you are between TAD (Route 38) and The Window (Route 49). The route starts two cracks right of the main crack of Cave (Route 42).

PITCH 1: Climb up and traverse right under a roof to the next crack. Pass the roof on the right and belay above it (150 feet, 5.10d). **PITCH 2:** Continue up the crack until you can belay among some bushes (150 feet, 5.11c). **FINISH:** Climb up to a roof and pass it on the left, then continue up to the summit (160 feet, 5.9+). Or you can belay above the roof at a good spot and scramble up to the summit from there.

SUGGESTED EQUIPMENT: Full set of Hexentrics and Stoppers with extra Stoppers of all sizes.

NOTE: The aid route started one crack right of the start of the free route.

45. BEELZEBUB II, 5.10b

FIRST ASCENT: September 24, 1976, by Dennis Horning and Frank Sanders. **APPROACH:** Follow the South Face Approach, then traverse right on The Ramp until you are below the south edge of The Window (Route 49). This route passes through the first roof left of the group of roofs on the east side of the Tower.

PITCH 1: Flake. Begin below a prominent flake just right of the base of the crack. After a few face moves follow a hand-jam crack to the top of the flake. Belay at the bolts (55 feet, 5.8). **PITCH 2:** Dihedral. From the top of the flake, step left into the crack and continue through the dihedral. Above the first dihedral traverse left into a smaller dihedral for a few moves, then back into the crack and up to a good belay ledge. There are some fixed pins in this pitch. Belay at the bolts on the left ledge (140 feet, 5.8). **PITCH 3:** Roof. Continue up the crack. The crux is about 12 feet below the roof. An irremovable pin is at the bottom of the roof. After the roof is negotiated on the right face, climb above a bush and belay at the bolts on the left ledge (110 feet, 5.10b). **PITCH 4:** Meadows. Follow the most prominent line. After a large ledge one can pick up the third-class Standard Meadows Finish by going 25 feet left (125 feet, 5.9). **FINISH:** Standard Meadows Finish.

SUGGESTED EQUIPMENT: #1 to #9 Hexentrics, #2 to #12 Stoppers, and extra small Stoppers.

46. LET ME GO WILD II, 5.12b

FIRST ASCENT: October 21, 1978, by Steve Gardiner, Terry Rypkema, and Frank

Sanders as the aid route Tower Classic (III, 5.7, A2). **FIRST FREE ASCENT:** of Pitch 1 — September 20, 1980, by Mark Smedley and Jim Black; of Pitch 2 — August 15, 1984, by Todd Skinner and Beth Wald. **APPROACH:** Same as The Window (Route 49). This route is in the first beautiful, right-facing dihedral to the left of The Window roofs.

PITCH 1: Climb up this delightful combination pitch (hand crack, perfect liebacking, face climbing, and thin fingers) which includes a few good rests. Hang a belay at the pins above a horizontal crack (140 feet, 5.10d). **PITCH 2:** Continue up on absolutely incredible, thin stemming, face climbing, and liebacking with a great deal of 5.11 leading up to a stemming crux. This is aesthetic climbing with four fixed pins and superb Stopper placements for the entire length. Belay at a cluster of pins below some loose blocks (90 feet, 5.12b). **FINISH:** Todd Skinner recommends rappelling off, or you can easily climb the same crack to the summit on Pitch 3 of Tower Classic, Route 47 (165 feet, 5.7).

SUGGESTED EQUIPMENT: Pitch 1 — small and medium Stoppers and #1 Friends. Pitch 2 — many small Stoppers, quick draws, and RPs. Take larger pieces to go to the top.

NOTE: Todd Skinner says, "One of the most classic corners of this grade in America." He rates this a three-star climb.

47. TOWER CLASSIC III, 5.7, A2 (5.12 free)

FIRST ASCENT: October 21, 1978, by Steve Gardiner, Terry Rypkema, and Frank Sanders (III, 5.7, A2). **FIRST FREE ASCENT:** of the first two pitches — August 15, 1984, by Todd Skinner and Beth Wald. **APPROACH:** Take the South Face Approach and The Ramp to The Window (Route 49). The route is in the first right-facing dihedral left of The Window roofs.

PITCH 1: This has been climbed free as Let Me Go Wild, Route 46, Pitch 1 (140 feet, 5.10d). **PITCH 2:** This has been climbed free as Let Me Go Wild, Pitch 2 (90 feet, 5.12b). **PITCH 3:** Continue straight up the crack to a belay at the end of your rope (165 feet, 5.7). **FINISH:** Walk to the top.

SUGGESTED EQUIPMENT: Same as Let Me Go Wild.

48. ANIMAL CRACKER LAND I, 5.12b

FIRST ASCENT: August 1, 1984, by Todd Skinner and Beth Wald. **APPROACH:** Same as Beelzebub (Route 45). Start one crack right of Beelzebub, which is Let Me Go Wild (Route 46) free, or the old aid route Tower Classic (Route 47). On the left edge of The Window (Route 49) is a striking, finger-size fracture crack on an overhanging column face. This is the route.

PITCH 1: Enter this thin crack from the left on lieback edges after a blind #1-1/2 Friend placement. Continue on sustained, strenuous locks and stems to a chockstone with a ring angle. Don't clip into the pin as it exists only to help keep the chockstone in place. Continue until you come to the end of the finger crack and then make a move left into a right-leaning hand crack. Continue up to a hanging belay (155 feet, 5.12b). **FINISH:** Rappel off.

SUGGESTED EQUIPMENT: Many small and medium Stoppers and also #1, #1-1/2, and #2 Friends.

NOTE: This crack is wild and very unlike any other cracks at the Tower according to Todd Skinner.

49. THE WINDOW IV, 5.6, A4

FIRST ASCENT: August 20, 1964, by Royal Robbins and Peter Robinson. This climb took 10 hours and 60 pitons the first time it was done. **APPROACH:** Take the South Face Approach to the base of the Meadows Rappel and traverse The Ramp to the right all the way around to the base of The Window, or leave the Tower Trail below The Window and climb onto the shoulder fourth class and easy fifth class to the base of the climb. Plan for a long day.

PITCH 1: Take the first crack right of the innermost right-facing dihedral on the left side of The Window. Climb up on easy placements. The belay is in slings suspended from good pitons (140 feet, A2). Bring a good selection of smaller nuts as much of this section can be done clean. **PITCH 2:** This pitch gets progressively more difficult until the first ceiling is reached. Here one can get in some solid pins. Passing the two roofs is the crux of the climb. The roof is now almost completely fixed. Pins lead over the second roof to a belay in slings 25 feet higher. Bring small nuts and RPs for use in pin scars. Bring some Friends (#1 to #3) for the crack past the roofs, as rope drag makes free climbing this stretch difficult (150 feet, A4). **FINISH:** Traverse left one crack and climb 25 feet before returning to the original crack, which is followed to the summit (150 feet, 5.6).

SUGGESTED EQUIPMENT: A good selection of blades, including Lost Arrows, short thicks and short thins, small to medium knifeblades, Leepers, SMCs, baby and long angles, and lots of tie-off loops and carabiners. Also, small nuts, RPs, and Friends.

50. LUCIFER'S LEDGES III, A3

FIRST ASCENT: October 29, 1978, by Frank Sanders, Steve Gardiner, Terry Rypkema, and Mark Brackin. **APPROACH:** Take the South Face Approach and The Ramp to below The Window (Route 49). Continue past the start of The Window to a point below the rightmost roof of The Window series. The next column face is broken badly and leads to a roof higher than The Window roof. The route lies in the right-hand crack of this broken face.

PITCH 1: Climb on varying aid to an established hanging belay (155 feet, A2+). **PITCH 2:** Continue in the same crack on more difficult placements through some sections of very loose and unappealing rock to a standing ledge where a nut and pin anchor is found (120 feet, A3). **PITCH 3:** Climb on questionable placements to a point where the crack ends and a large, blank wall is above (50 feet, A3). **FINISH:** Rappel from here.

SUGGESTED EQUIPMENT: A full rack of Stoppers and Hexentrics, with pitons ranging from RURPs to bongs.

NOTE: This route is not recommended.

51. SATAN'S STAIRWAY III, 5.8, A3

FIRST ASCENT: July 4, 1984, by Steve Gardiner, Joe Sears, Chris Engle, and Dave Johnson. **APPROACH:** Same as The Window (Route 49). At the right edge of The Window roofs you will see a higher roof, then another roof to the right at the same level as The Window overhangs. The right-hand crack below this roof is in a dihedral and is the route. It is one crack right of Lucifer's Ledges (Route 50) and three cracks left of Witchie (Route 52).

58
58
47
56
57
53
48
58
52
54
55
56
50
46
49
51

PITCH 1: Scramble on blocks just to the right of the actual route to a point where a six-inch ledge traverses into the crack. From there, climb on mixed free and aid to a fixed hanging belay on pins and nuts. The crux is a small roof about 120 feet up. Turn this roof on a sky hook (145 feet, 5.8, A2+). **PITCH 2:** Continue on sustained thin aid (using several tie-offs) up the same crack to a fixed hanging belay (140 feet, A3). **FINISH:** Rappel from here.

SUGGESTED EQUIPMENT: A full rack of Stoppers, Hexentrics, and pitons, including many knifeblades, tie-offs, RURPs, and at least one sky hook.

NOTE: It appears that the roof above the rappel point may have a crack through it, but a lengthy series of bashies or bolts would be needed to get there.

52. WITCHIE III, 5.10a

FIRST ASCENT: August 31, 1975, by Geoffrey Conley and John Pearson. **APPROACH:** Take the East Buttress Approach to the top of the buttress and traverse left of Casper College (Route 54) two cracks. This is Witchie and also the start of Crocodile (Route 53).

PITCH 1: After climbing 30 feet to a roof, work left around the corner to a hand and fist crack. A couple of bushes make the crux of the first pitch. Belay at the bolts on the left side (80 feet, 5.9). **PITCH 2:** Follow this open-book, left-leaning crack with jams from finger to hand size (160 feet, 5.10a). **PITCH 3:** Jam and stem until the crack becomes a chimney which you climb to a column top on your right (90 feet, 5.7). **FINISH:** Step left to a shallow chimney and climb to the summit (70 feet, 5.5).

SUGGESTED EQUIPMENT: #2 to #12 Stoppers with extra #3 to #12s, and a full set of Hexentrics.

53. CROCODILE III, 5.10d

FIRST ASCENT: July 2, 1976, by Dennis Horning and Curt Haire. **APPROACH:** Same as Witchie (Route 52). The line goes to the overhang under the crocodile's head, turns it on the right, and continues up the crack between Witchie and Casper College (Route 54).

PITCH 1: Climb up the start of Witchie, an easy dihedral about 30 feet, to the nose of the Crocodile. Turn the overhang on the right (crux) and continue up the thin crack (there's a fixed Leeper here) which widens to a chimney, then narrows to a hand jam up to a bush. Belay at the bolts (75 feet, 5.10d). **PITCH 2:** Jam the crack directly up from the belay to a good belay stance atop the right-hand column (155 feet, 5.7). **PITCH 3:** Climb the leftmost crack (off width but not too difficult) from the ledge to the top of the left-hand column (about 90 feet). Traverse right to another crack, and continue up it for another 50 feet to a belay on a good ledge (150 feet, 5.7). **FINISH:** Third class to the summit.

SUGGESTED EQUIPMENT: #1 to #11 Hexentrics with extra #7 to #9s, and #3 to #12 Stoppers with extra #7s and #8s.

54. CASPER COLLEGE III, 5.10d

FIRST ASCENT: June 7, 1956, by Dud McReynolds, Walt Bailey, David Sturde-

Opposite: East Face

vant, and Bruce Smith (III, 5.7, A2). **FIRST FREE ASCENT:** June 1, 1979, by Jim Beyer and Dennis Horning. **APPROACH:** Take the East Buttress Approach until you reach a large platform on the buttress below the vertical columns. Look up from here and you will see a large crack with two gooseberry bushes growing out of it, running up between the faces to two yellow columns. This is Gooseberry Jam (Route 56). The Casper College route starts two cracks left of it and has a few fixed pins.

PITCH 1: Climb this crack until you reach a good belay ledge and belay from the bolts on the right (150 feet, 5.10d). The crux of the climb is about 70 feet up where the crack thins and the face bulges. **PITCH 2:** Continue up the same gradually widening crack and pass an overhang on your right about 50 feet up. From here on, the column and crack to the right make the free climbing easier. Stop and belay from a good ledge just left of the crack (145 feet, 5.7). **FINISH:** Climb and scramble easily to the summit (85 feet, 5.3).

SUGGESTED EQUIPMENT: #1 to #8 Hexentrics, several #3 to #12 Stoppers, and runners.

55. BURNING DAYLIGHT II, 5.10b

FIRST ASCENT: October 30, 1977, by Dennis Horning and Mike Todd. **APPROACH:** Take the East Buttress Approach. This route lies one crack left of Gooseberry Jam (Route 56) and one crack right of Casper College (Route 54).

PITCH 1: Ascend the left-facing dihedral, moving past a crackless overhanging section to a strenuous finger-jam crack leading through a roof. Above the roof, the going is somewhat easier. Belay at the platform on top of the columns (160 feet, 5.10b). **PITCH 2:** Above the platform are four roofs. Climb the second from the left crack to a column top on the left side of the crack. The crux is going through the roofs. Same as Belle Fourche Buttress (Route 58), Pitch 3 (150 feet, 5.8). **FINISH:** Work up and to the right for an easy finish (100 feet, 5.4).

SUGGESTED EQUIPMENT: #1 to #8 Hexentrics and #3 to #12 Stoppers with extra #8 to #12s.

56. GOOSEBERRY JAM III, 5.9–

FIRST ASCENT: July 23, 1959, by Bob Kamps and Don Yestness. **APPROACH:** Take the East Buttress Approach. Look up and you will see a large crack with two gooseberry bushes growing out of it, running up between the faces of the two yellow columns. This is the route and it is also two cracks right of Casper College (Route 54).

PITCH 1: Climb onto the flakes at the base, or lieback up a large slab for about 20 feet. Proceed up the off-width jam crack, climbing up a large flake and passing the first bush. Lieback or jam up and past the second bush where the steepness eases a little and the crack begins to widen so that climbing is a little easier. Continue up to a large belay ledge (150 feet, 5.9–). **PITCH 2:** Continue straight up on easy climbing about 30 feet where you will be on a ledge under some roofs. Traverse left two cracks under the roofs. Climb past the roof to a good belay ledge on your left (50 feet, 5.4). **PITCH 3:** Same as Casper College, Pitch 2. Climb the gradually widening crack and stop to belay from either the top of the column on your right or on a ledge to your left about 10 to 15 feet higher (125 feet, 5.7). **FINISH:** Same as Casper College finish (80 feet, 5.3).

SUGGESTED EQUIPMENT: A set each of Hexentrics and Stoppers. Friends help. Take several 3- to 4-inch pieces.

57. GOOSEBERRY JAM—PETERSON VARIATION III, 5.10a

FIRST ASCENT: May ?, 1978, by Don Peterson. **APPROACH:** Follow the East Buttress Approach and climb Gooseberry Jam (Route 56) to the large ledge below the main roofs.

PITCH 1: From the top of Gooseberry Jam (Pitch 1) climb the right crack above you. This is one crack right of Belle Fourche Buttress (Route 58). Climb up through some bushes and the bulges above. Belay at a large column-top ledge (150 feet, 5.10a). **FINISH:** You can climb and scramble straight up or easily traverse right and up to the summit.

SUGGESTED EQUIPMENT: Same as Gooseberry Jam.

NOTE: Don Peterson was belayed from below while he climbed this Peterson Variation.

58. BELLE FOURCHE BUTTRESS III, 5.10b

FIRST ASCENT: May 28, 1961, by Don Ryan and Gary Cole (III, 5.8, A3). **FIRST FREE ASCENT:** October 16, 1977, by Dennis Horning and Dave Rasmussen. **APPROACH:** Take the East Buttress Route to the base of Gooseberry Jam (Route 56).

PITCH 1: Start up Gooseberry Jam, then traverse right and belay from two bolts on top of a large block. The route follows the first crack on the north side of the buttress (30 feet, 5.6). The original aid climb started at the very base of the crack. **PITCH 2:** Traverse right to a hand and finger crack and follow it to the top of the buttress (155 feet, 5.10b). The crux comes after 10 feet of hand jams where the crack constricts to 20 feet of finger-size jams leading to a rest. Strenuous hand jams complete this pitch. **PITCH 3:** Climb two cracks left above you (two cracks right of Casper College, Route 54). Climb easily to the roofs and continue up the crack to a belay on a column top (150 feet, 5.8). **FINISH:** Easy fourth-class climbing and scrambling to the summit directly up or up and right.

SUGGESTED EQUIPMENT: #1 to #8 Hexentrics, #3 to #12 Stoppers with extra #8 to #12s, and #1/2 to #3 Friends help.

Northeast Face

59. TWO LEFT SHOES III, 5.8, A1

FIRST ASCENT: July 27, 1978, solo by Jim Beyer (III, 5.8, A1). **APPROACH:** Take the East Buttress Approach until you are almost on top of the buttress. The route is located one crack to the right of Belle Fourche Buttress. Scramble up to the belay below a short vertical wall.

60
60
58
59
60
59
62
63
61
64
65
66
67
68
69
66
70

PITCH 1: Climb the short wall and step left. Climb up the right-facing dihedral to the top of the flakes. Climb the hand crack above to get a high nut in, then drop down and face climb to the right and belay above the traverse (120 feet, 5.8). **PITCH 2:** Continue up the crack and bear right into the groove. Free climb as high as possible, then traverse on aid from the groove to the crack on the left face and then left to the face crack outside the groove (90 feet, 5.8, A1). About five points of aid, mostly horizontal pitons. **PITCH 3:** Aid up to a belay just right of a roof (75 feet, 5.6, A1). **PITCH 4:** Mixed free and aid leads to an easy chimney. Belay atop the pedestal on your left (150 feet, 5.8+, A1). **FINISH:** Fourth class to the top.

SUGGESTED EQUIPMENT: A big blade, six horizontals, two or three of each angle up to 1-1/2 inches, and a set each of Stoppers and Hexentrics.

NOTE: Much of this has been climbed free as Dump Watt (Route 60). Jim Beyer said, "The route is named for a mistake I had to live with."

60. DUMP WATT II, 5.10b

FIRST ASCENT: August 29, 1981, by Mark Smedley, Eric Rhicard, and Dave Larsen. **APPROACH:** Follow the East Buttress Approach. This route is one crack right of Belle Fourche (Route 58) and starts on the old aid route Two Left Shoes (Route 59).

PITCH 1: Belay fairly high. Stay on Two Left Shoes until it goes left, then climb straight up the finger and hand crack which again becomes Two Left Shoes. Continue up to the bolts for a belay at the bottom of an acute dihedral (150 feet, 5.9+). **PITCH 2:** Continue up on Two Left Shoes until it traverses left and you go straight up the acute dihedral to a horizontal ledge leading left. Hand traverse left to good ledges, then climb the finger and hand crack (crux) to a small bush that is below and left of the big overhang that tops the acute dihedral. Hang a belay here (135 feet, 5.10b). **PITCH 3:** Climb the crack up through a chimney to the top of a pillar on your left (150 feet, 5.9). **FINISH:** Same as Two Left Shoes.

SUGGESTED EQUIPMENT: #1 to #8 Hexentrics with extra #9s and #10s, and #3 to #12 Stoppers, with extra small to medium sizes.

61. THE CHUTE I, 5.10d

FIRST ASCENT: July 11, 1982, by Dennis Horning and Hollis Marriott. **APPROACH:** Take the Northeast Buttress Approach until you reach the constriction (Hourglass) between the East Buttress Approach and the Northeast Buttress. From here climb up to the base of the climb above you and between the buttresses. The crack is the left side of a long, leaning column in the innermost part of the cove between the two buttresses.

PITCH 1: Climb up the left side of The Chute Column using finger and hand jams, stemming, and face climbing. The first 20 feet is loose. Finish climbing the top off width to the belay bolts at the column top. A 5.9 off-width move at the top can be protected with a #4 Friend. Belay at the top bolts (160 feet, 5.10d). **FINISH:** Rappel from here.

SUGGESTED EQUIPMENT: #1 to #8 Hexentrics, #3 to #12 Stoppers, a #4 Friend, and many extra small to medium pieces.

Opposite: Northeast Face

62. SEE YOU IN SOHO I, 5.12b

FIRST ASCENT: August 14, 1985, by Todd Skinner and Beth Wald. **APPROACH:** Follow the Northeast Buttress Approach until you are directly below The Chute (Route 61). Climb up to the start of The Chute which gets you to the pitch above. The route starts one crack left of the top of The Chute Column.

PITCH 1: Same as The Chute, Pitch 1 (160 feet, 5.10d). **PITCH 2:** From the top of The Chute Column, step left one crack and climb through a roof to a thin finger crack. Follow this narrowing crack to a two-pin hanging belay at the base of the broken rock (130 feet, 5.12b). **FINISH:** Rappel from here.

SUGGESTED EQUIPMENT: Many #2 to #5 RPs and small to medium Stoppers, with one quick draw for a fixed pin.

63. NITRO EXPRESS II, 5.11c

FIRST ASCENT: July 27, 1985, by Steve Petro, Beth Wald, and Todd Skinner. **APPROACH:** Follow the Northeast Buttress Approach until you are directly below The Chute (Route 61). Climb up to the start of The Chute which gets you to Nitro Express above.

PITCH 1: Same as The Chute, Pitch 1 (160 feet, 5.10d). **PITCH 2:** From the top of The Chute Column, climb up the finger crack above you. This is an interesting pitch with intricate face climbing, some stems, and very thin fingertip "cranks." A thin face move 40 feet up is the crux for the pitch. Continue up to a hanging belay at the bolts (80 feet, 5.11c). **FINISH:** Rappel from the bolts.

SUGGESTED EQUIPMENT: Three each #3, #4 and #5 RPs. Also take many small to medium wired Stoppers and #1/2 to #1-1/2 Friends.

NOTE: Occasional stances and good protection make this a two-star route.

64. KAMA SUTRA III, 5.10a

FIRST ASCENT: September 28, 1976, by Dennis Horning, Cody Paulson, and Frank Sanders. **APPROACH:** Take the Northeast Buttress Approach and start at the base of Suchness (Route 65). Most of the route lies one crack left of Suchness. The first climb started farther left, but that approach is no longer used.

PITCH 1: Begin left of the crack just below two weathered tree stumps. Climb up through a bush, and belay where this route starts left to Suchness (70 feet, 5.5). **PITCH 2:** Traverse left above this ledge using small holds and friction and ascend the bushy crack to a comfortable belay stance on a broken column on the left (130 feet, 5.7). **PITCH 3:** Climb down several feet and traverse right into a crack. The first 70 feet of this crack is hand jamming. About 15 feet above the bush is a fixed bong where a good hanging belay anchor can be set (100 feet, 5.10a). **PITCH 4:** The next section of crack passing the horizontal crack on the right is fist jamming; the crack above widens to a squeeze chimney leading to a belay ledge on top of the column (110 feet, 5.9). **FINISH:** Continue up the same crack to the top (150 feet, 5.6). You can also take the right crack to the summit.

SUGGESTED EQUIPMENT: #1 to #8 Hexentrics and a set of #3 to #12 Stoppers. Also a 5-inch tube chock and five 2- to 3-1/2-inch pieces.

NOTE: Kama Sutra is the route of a hundred and one positions, each one harder than the last.

65. SUCHNESS III, 5.10b

FIRST ASCENT: June 2, 1974, by Dennis Horning and Paul Piana (III, 5.8, A1). **FIRST FREE ASCENT:** September 7, 1976, by Dennis Horning and Frank Sanders. **APPROACH:** Take the Northeast Buttress Approach. This crack is one crack left of Patent Pending (Route 66) at the midface level and is in the crack that goes between the two midface roofs.

PITCH 1: The pitch begins left of the crack just below two weathered tree stumps. Climb up through a bush and belay where Kama Sutra (Route 64) starts left (70 feet, 5.5). **PITCH 2:** Continue up the crack. About two-thirds of the way up, there is a tricky bulge. Just below the roof, traverse left to a thin sitting belay ledge (150 feet, 5.8). The belay anchor takes some rigging. **PITCH 3:** Climb over the four-foot roof which is the crux and protect with 2- to 3-inch pieces. The crack above the roof remains quite hard for about 12 feet. Continue up the crack, protecting with tube chocks and large hex nuts. Continue up past some natural chock rocks and belay at a good ledge on top of a large chock rock near the North Face tunnel (155 feet, 5.10b). **PITCH 4:** Chimney up to the top of a broken column, then traverse left to a crack and continue up the crack except to veer right around a bush (135 feet, 5.5). **FINISH:** Climb up to the summit in the crack above you (60 feet, 5.5).

SUGGESTED EQUIPMENT: A set each of Hexentrics and Stoppers, extra medium to large pieces, and six 3- to 4-inch pieces. A couple of tube chocks and large Friends help; also extra runners.

66. PATENT PENDING III, 5.8+

FIRST ASCENT: May 8, 1971, by Charles Bare and Jim Olson (III, 5.7, A1 or A2). **FIRST FREE ASCENT:** August 17, 1972, by Bruce K. Bright and Dennis Drayna. **APPROACH:** Take the Northeast Buttress Approach until you are on top of the east end of the buttress directly below three prominent roofs.

PITCH 1: Climb up face holds and the obvious crack through some bushes to a good belay ledge behind a large flake (120 feet, 5.5). If you belay high, it is 80 feet. **PITCH 2:** From the belay traverse up and left a short distance, then climb straight up to a belay ledge directly beneath an overhang (160 feet, 5.4), Teacher's Lounge. **PITCH 3:** Climb one crack left of Assembly Line (Route 67) through the overhang, which is the crux of the climb. Continue up this off-width crack and belay in the chimney below the tunnel (160 feet, 5.8+). **PITCH 4:** Continue up on easy climbing to the end of your rope and belay (150 to 160 feet, 5.6). **FINISH:** Easy scramble to the summit.

SUGGESTED EQUIPMENT: #1 to #8 Hexentrics, #3 to #12 Stoppers, and six 2-1/2 to 4-inch pieces.

NOTE: Instead of traversing left after Pitch 1, the original route probably went straight up to Teacher's Lounge.

67. ASSEMBLY LINE III, 5.9

FIRST ASCENT: May 18, 1975, by Dennis Horning and Judd Jennerjahn. **APPROACH:** Take the Northeast Buttress Approach until you are on top of the east end of the buttress directly below three prominent midface roofs.

PITCH 1: You can get to Teacher's Lounge, a large ledge below the overhangs, in one pitch if you tandem climb (180 feet if you start high). We recommend doing it in two pitches from the bottom. Climb, bushwack up a feasible crack to a good belay ledge behind a large flake (80 feet, 5.5). If you start low, it is 120 feet. **PITCH 2:** Climb up and traverse left one crack. Take this crack to Teacher's Lounge (160 feet, 5.5). **PITCH 3:** Face climb and stem to start this crack which is the long hand crack on the right side of the three roofs. The finger crux is near the bottom. Climb to the belay bolts on the left side of the crack (155 feet, 5.9). **PITCH 4:** Continue up the crack to a belay right below a roof (140 feet, 5.8). **FINISH:** Traverse left one crack and climb this easy crack to the summit.

SUGGESTED EQUIPMENT: A full set of Hexentrics and larger wired Stoppers, also runners. Be sure to take *extra* medium Hexentrics and large Stoppers.

NORTHEAST CORNER III, 5.7, A3

FIRST ASCENT: June 2, 1964, by Dean Moore and Paul Stettner. **APPROACH:** Same as Patent Pending (Route 66).

EXPLANATION: There is more than a little confusion as to the exact location of this aid route. Park Service records and recent contact with one of the original party could not definitely nail down the route. Contact with knowledgeable climbers has not helped much either. Most feel it is two cracks right of Assembly Line (Route 67) (now the free climb Surfer Girl, Route 68), but the route apparently changed cracks several times and is poorly defined. A M&CWTC route was most likely done earlier on part or much of this route. Neither of these routes is shown on our photo plots due to uncertainty.

68. SURFER GIRL II, 5.12c

FIRST ASCENT: See explanation under Note below. **FIRST FREE ASCENT:** July 14, 1984, by Todd Skinner and Beth Wald. **APPROACH:** Same as Assembly Line (Route 67). This route starts from Teacher's Lounge, a large ledge that is midface on the north side of the Tower. It is two cracks right of Assembly Line and one crack left of Maid in the Shaid (Route 69).

PITCHES 1 AND 2: Same as Patent Pending (Route 66), Pitches 1 and 2, or any other route that will get you to the Teacher's Lounge ledge. **PITCH 3:** Surfer Girl. This is a clean, enjoyable finger, face, and stemming problem with extremely good protection for most of the route. There are some fixed pins. Climb one crack left of Maid in the Shaid with very desperate and sustained flaring fingers. The crux of the climb is about 90 feet up. After this crux, the climbing is easy up to a bolt belay on the right column face (155 feet, 5.12c). **FINISH:** Rappel down; or you can go up and left to reach the top via Assembly Line or Patent Pending; or you can go up to your right and finish on Maid in the Shaid.

SUGGESTED EQUIPMENT: Many small and medium Stoppers with a few #1 Friends and runners. Bring a few larger pieces for the first two pitches and whatever you might need if you go higher.

NOTE: Two earlier aid routes, Northeast Corner and an M&CWTC, have been put up to the right of Assembly Line and a lot of confusion exists as to their locations. Sections of these routes may be part of what is now Surfer Girl. Todd Skinner did the crux of this route in the midst of a hailstorm using mad-dog motivation, he said.

69. MAID IN THE SHAID III, 5.11d

FIRST ASCENT: May 13, 1978, by Terry Rypkema, Frank Sanders, Steve Gardiner, and Debbie Berglund (III, 5.8, A2). **FIRST FREE ASCENT:** June 25, 1983, by Steve Hong, Andy Hong, and Karin Budding. **APPROACH:** Take the Northeast Buttress Approach. This route is three cracks right of Assembly Line (Route 67) and starts on the right side of Teacher's Lounge (rightmost crack).

PITCHES 1 AND 2: Climb New Wave (Route 70) or Broken Tree (Route 71) to Teacher's Lounge (200 feet, 5.10 a or b). **PITCH 3:** The start of the route is a classic, beautiful corner that is one of the purest stemming pitches at the Tower. The entire pitch is sustained with no real rests, but with good protection. Many small wired Stoppers are needed for the first half and small hand-size protection for the last half. Belay at two bolts on the left column face (165 feet, 5.11d). Many rappel from here, which makes it Grade II. **PITCH 4:** Chimney and jam to the end of your rope and belay on a large block (160 feet, 5.6). **FINISH:** Scramble to the top.

SUGGESTED EQUIPMENT: Three sets of RPs, multiple small to medium Stoppers and three or four # 1 and # 2 Friends (30 pieces in all).

NOTE: Steve Hong rates this a three-star route on a scale of one to three.

70. NEW WAVE I, 5.10a

FIRST ASCENT: June 10, 1982, by Dave Larsen and Dennis Horning. **APPROACH:** Take the Northeast Buttress Approach. This route starts under Teacher's Lounge ledge at the same point Broken Tree (Route 71) starts.

PITCH 1: Start up and traverse up and left two cracks. This is the New Wave route. Work up the jam crack and face until you come to the small belay ledge at the bolts on your right (100 feet, 5.7). **PITCH 2:** Continue up the crack to the crux of the climb, which is protected by a bolt on the left. Step up right on friction only until you can get your hands back in the crack. Finish on mixed climbing to Teacher's Lounge (140 feet, 5.10a). **FINISH:** Rappel down the way you came, or go to the summit via any of several routes above.

SUGGESTED EQUIPMENT: # 1 to # 7 Hexentrics, # 3 to # 12 Stoppers, and any other items you may need if you go to the summit.

NOTE: This is a very good route.

71. BROKEN TREE I, 5.10b

FIRST ASCENT: June 22, 1982, by Dennis Horning and Dave Larsen. **APPROACH:** Follow the Northeast Buttress Approach just around a corner past Assembly Line (Route 67). The start is the same as New Wave (Route 70) but follows the crack above the broken tree you have to step over. This is also just left of the Everlasting Column (Route 72).

PITCH 1: Climb the crack, in a left-facing dihedral, that is the westernmost crack to achieve the Teacher's Lounge ledge. There is easy climbing to a double bolt belay (80 feet, 5.7). **PITCH 2:** Climb this varied crack with thin stemming, some rotten rock, and a crux that is a 15-foot finger crack at the top. Belay at the Teacher's Lounge bolts (140 feet, 5.10b). **FINISH:** Rappel from here, or climb any of several other routes above to the summit.

SUGGESTED EQUIPMENT: Use a variety of nuts but mostly small nuts and Stoppers.

72. EVERLASTING I, 5.10c

FIRST ASCENT: August 13, 1983, by Dennis Horning and Dave Larsen. **APPROACH:** Take the Northeast Buttress Approach past New Wave to the base of the Everlasting Column. Everlasting is between Broken Tree (Route 71) and Sympathy for the Devil (Route 74) and is one of two face routes on the Tower protected by bolts. Belay from the very large pine tree at the base of the route.

PITCH 1: Climb up the low-angle crack until it thins. Now traverse left and up until you can traverse back right to a small belay ledge at the belay bolts (155 feet, 5.8+). **PITCH 2:** Traverse up and left until you get into the corner, then move back up and right on airy moves to the face of the column. From here face climb the center of the column until you reach its top. Belay at the bolts here (150 feet, 5.10c). Bolts protect this pitch. **FINISH:** It is recommended that you rappel off here. You could attempt the difficult crack above, which is Hollow Men (Route 73), 5.12c, the most difficult pitch climbed on the Tower.

SUGGESTED EQUIPMENT (for Everlasting only): Eleven quick draws and medium Stoppers.

73. HOLLOW MEN II, 5.12c

FIRST ASCENT: As Sympathy for the Devil (Route 74), September 5, 1981, by Frank Sanders and Chris Engle (III, 5.9, A2). **FIRST FREE ASCENT:** August 6, 1985, by Todd Skinner and Beth Wald. **APPROACH:** Follow the Northeast Buttress Approach to the base of the climb. The Hollow Men pitch starts from the top of the Everlasting Column (Route 72).

PITCHES 1 AND 2: You can reach the start of the pitch by climbing any route that gets you to the Teacher's Lounge ledge where a short pitch takes you to the base of Hollow Men; this was recommended by Todd Skinner. Or you can climb Everlasting, Sympathy for the Devil (Route 74), or Back to Montana (Route 75) to get on top of the Everlasting Column. **PITCH 3:** Hollow Men. Climb up this desperate and sustained blank corner with a noticeable lack of fingerlocks. This is a stemming problem with numerous 5.12 sections. Belay at the bolts under the roof (140 feet, 5.12c). **FINISH:** Rappel off or continue up on Sympathy for the Devil (140 feet, 5.9).

SUGGESTED EQUIPMENT: First ascent party had five #1 RPs, fourteen #2 RPs and five each of #3 to #5 RPs; also a few small Stoppers and a #1 Friend.

NOTE: Hollow Men was the most difficult pitch on the Tower at the time of this writing.

74. SYMPATHY FOR THE DEVIL III, 5.9, A2 (5.12c free)

FIRST ASCENT: September 5, 1981, by Frank Sanders and Chris Engle (III, 5.10d, A2). **FIRST FREE ASCENT:** of the Back to Montana (Route 75) portion — June 27, 1982, by Dennis Horning and Monte Cooper. **FIRST FREE ASCENT:** of

Northeast Face (left) and North Face

Pitch 3 as Hollow Men (Route 73) — August 6, 1985, by Todd Skinner and Beth Wald. **APPROACH:** Use the Northeast Buttress Approach until you are on the right (west) side of the Everlasting Column (Route 72). This route starts one crack left of Mystic and the Mulchers (Route 76). Belay at the tree, in the crack, that is two cracks right of the route.

PITCH 1: Climb the crack to where it pinches in, then mantle and climb the face on the left. Belay at the Back to Montana starting bolts (160 feet, 5.8). **PITCH 2:** This pitch has been climbed free as Back to Montana, Pitch 2. Belay at the bolts on top of the Everlasting Column (150 feet, 5.10d). **PITCH 3:** This has been climbed free as Hollow Men, Pitch 3 (140 feet, 5.12c). **PITCH 4:** Climb up and traverse left under the roof. Keep on until you can set a belay (140 feet, 5.9). **FINISH:** Climb to the top (40 feet, 5.4).

SUGGESTED EQUIPMENT: Hexentrics, Stoppers, #1 Friend, and many Lost Arrows and angles. See the free-climb descriptions for equipment used on them.

75. BACK TO MONTANA II, 5.10d

FIRST ASCENT: As Sympathy for the Devil (Route 74), September 5, 1981, by Frank Sanders and Chris Engle (III, 5.9, A2). **FIRST FREE ASCENT:** June 27, 1982, by Dennis Horning and Monte Cooper. **APPROACH:** Same as Everlasting (Route 72).

PITCH 1: Same as Everlasting, Pitch 1 (155 feet, 5.8+), or Sympathy for the Devil, Pitch 1 (160 feet, 5.8). Belay at the bolts. **PITCH 2:** Back to Montana. Just above the bolts traverse right to a crack in a right-facing dihedral. Climb this very thin crack with fingers where they fit, and stem where they don't, to the top of the broken column and belay at the bolts there (150 feet, 5.10d). **FINISH:** Rappel from here or continue up on Hollow Men, Route 73 (140 feet, 5.12c) and Sympathy for the Devil (140 feet, 5.9) to the summit.

SUGGESTED EQUIPMENT: #1 to #8 Hexentrics and #3 to #12 Stoppers. Also a #1 Friend and #1 to #3 RPs.

North Face

76. MYSTIC AND THE MULCHERS I, 5.8−

FIRST ASCENT: July 27, 1985, by Jim Schlinkmann, Dick Guilmette, "Barney" Fisher, and Mateo Pee Pee. **APPROACH:** Same as McCarthy North Face (Route 80). The climb is three main cracks left of Pitch 1 of McCarthy North Face and two cracks right of Pitch 1 of Back to Montana (Route 75) or two cracks right of the start of Sympathy for the Devil (Route 74). The climb starts at a pine tree in the crack at the base of the climb.

PITCH 1: Climb the finger crack and face for 150 feet to a three-bolt belay (150 feet, 5.8−). The crux is near the end of the pitch and is protected by a bolt. This pitch has many good face holds and rests. Good protection. **FINISH:** Rappel from the bolts.

SUGGESTED EQUIPMENT: Many wired Rocks, RPs, #2 to #5 Hexentrics, #1, #1-1/2, and #3 Friends, and sliders.

77. NEVERLASTING I, 5.9−

FIRST ASCENT: August 26, 1985, by David Kozak and Denny Hochwender. **APPROACH:** Same as McCarthy North Face (Route 80). The pitch begins in the shallow dihedral one crack right of Mystic and the Mulchers (Route 76) and one crack left of Leaping Lizards (Route 78).

PITCH 1: Climb the shallow dihedral and then the face above to a stance between Mystic and the Mulchers and Leaping Lizards. Traverse left from here to the single bolt on Mystic and the Mulchers (it is more difficult if you traverse higher) and climb to the bolts that finish Mystic and the Mulchers (150 feet, 5.9−). **FINISH:** Rappel from here.

SUGGESTED EQUIPMENT: Take many small wires, RPs, small Stoppers, and a #1-1/2 Friend.

78. LEAPING LIZARDS I, 5.10a

FIRST ASCENT: As Jumpin' Jack Flash, August 29, 1981, by Frank Sanders and Dale Chamberlain (III, 5.7, A2). **FIRST FREE ASCENT:** August 3, 1985, by Carl Coy and Mark Jacobs. **APPROACH:** Take the Northeast Buttress Approach until you are below McCarthy North Face (Route 80). Belay high, just above a tree that is a few feet left of the start of McCarthy North Face.

PITCH 1: Follow the crack up on thin stemming moves. The crux is midway up the pitch. Near the end, traverse out to the left to belay from some bolts at a small ledge (100 feet, 5.10). **PITCH 2:** Utilize thin crack climbing and face moves for this pitch. Climb up and right to the original crack and then traverse up and left over a series of three small ledges to the left crack. Follow this crack up past the McCarthy roof until you can traverse back right to a hanging belay at the Daredevil Index bolts (Route 79) (100 feet, 5.10). **FINISH:** Rappel off or climb Daredevil Index directly above (5.12a); you can go to the summit from there on McCarthy North Face.

SUGGESTED EQUIPMENT: RPs, wired Stoppers, and #1-1/2, #2-1/2, and #3 Friends.

NOTE: This is rated a two-star route. Some of the last 40 feet on Pitch 2 is probably on Daredevil Index.

79. DAREDEVIL INDEX III, 5.12a

FIRST ASCENT: As Jumpin' Jack Flash, August 29, 1981, by Frank Sanders and Dale Chamberlain (III, 5.7, A2). **FIRST FREE ASCENT:** June 18, 1985, by Paul Piana and Steve Petro. **APPROACH:** Same as McCarthy North Face (Route 80). The route starts on McCarthy North Face at the bolts under the McCarthy roof.

PITCH 1: Same as McCarthy North Face, Pitch 1. **PITCH 2:** Traverse left, and utilize the next two cracks and the area between for climbing and protection. Climb this insecure and poorly protected pitch to the hanging belay at the bolts and one piton (40 feet, 5.9+). There is as much face climbing on the pitch as there is fingertip crack climbing. A #2 Friend halfway up the pitch is the only reliable piece to use. **PITCH 3:** Continue up these desperate #1 to #3 RP-size cracks where protection is hard to place. There are no jams, so you have to climb on fingertips, palming, lay-away moves, and painful stemming. The crux is "enduro" technical stemming three-quarters of the way up this pitch. Set up a hanging belay at the bolts under the roof (155 feet, 5.12a). **FINISH:** Rappelling is recommended, but you can traverse right 10 feet to McCarthy North Face and go to the summit on that. At the belay/rappel you will find carabiners with their gates epoxied shut that you can use for belay/rappel anchors.

SUGGESTED EQUIPMENT: Take at least four each #1 to #3 RPs, two #0.5 Tri-cams, one #1 Tri-cam, one #1 Friend, one #10 Stopper, two #5 and #6 Stoppers, and many #1 to #3 Stoppers. A #2 Friend for Pitch 2, and quick draws for the bolts.

NOTE: There are six bolts and five fixed pitons in Pitch 3.

80. McCARTHY NORTH FACE III, 5.11a

FIRST ASCENT: August 5, 1957, by Jim McCarthy and John Rupley (III, 5.7, A2). **FIRST FREE ASCENT:** May 28, 1978, by Dennis Horning and Frank Sanders. **APPROACH:** Take the Northeast Buttress Approach. When you get onto the buttress, continue west around a corner past Everlasting (Route 72) until you are 200 feet below a main roof. Third or fourth class up about 50 feet to a six-inch diameter tree and belay from a small ledge to its right, just below some friction.

PITCH 1: Climb the steep friction and right crack, passing two small bushes and a small bulge. Climb into a dihedral by making use of ledges on the left side, then get back into the crack. Climb past a small roof and over a loose block to a finger crack in the dihedral. Climb directly up the finger crack to a sloping belay ledge directly under the large roof. Belay at the bolts (165 feet, 5.8+). **PITCH 2:** Climb over the right side of the roof and continue up on the sustained finger crack (shallow) to a belay at the bolts (120 feet, 5.11a). **PITCH 3:** Continue up the thin hand-to-hand crack above to a small belay stance at some bolts (120 feet, 5.9). **PITCH 4:** Continue up through a chimney and to the end of your rope (140 feet, 5.6). **FINISH:** Scramble to the top.

SUGGESTED EQUIPMENT: #1 to #8 Hexentrics and lots of #3 to #12 Stoppers, with Friends and runners for the fixed pins on the first two pitches.

NOTE: Climbers are not recommending the bolts at the end of Pitch 3, so you should set up your own belay a little lower or higher.

81. McCARTHY'S BROTHER II, 5.10a

FIRST ASCENT: June 15, 1985, by Dennis Horning and Jim Schlinkmann. **APPROACH:** Take the Northeast Buttress Approach and continue west onto the Northwest Buttress just past McCarthy North Face (Route 80). The route is between McCarthy North Face and Emotional Rescue (Route 82).

PITCH 1: Start in the rightmost of two thin cracks on the arête. Belay low if you wish. Work your way up the thin crack, and gradually traverse left on face holds to the semihanging belay at the bolts (80 feet, 5.8). **PITCH 2:** Face climb on moderate 5.7 to 5.9 past five bolts. Climb the crux the last few feet on face holds to the bolts for a hanging belay (120 feet, 5.10a). **FINISH:** Rappel from the bolts.

SUGGESTED EQUIPMENT: Pitch 1 — RPs and small to medium Stoppers. Pitch 2 — five quick draws (for bolts), small to medium Stoppers, and RPs.

NOTE: Protection is listed as fair. Beware of loose rock on Pitch 2, especially a large flake midway in the pitch. The route could use more cleaning.

82. EMOTIONAL RESCUE III, 5.7, A3+

FIRST ASCENT: May 21, 1981, by Frank Sanders and Chris Engle. **APPROACH:** Use the Northeast Buttress Approach until you are right (west) of McCarthy North Face (Route 80), just left of Klondike (Route 85). The route goes up the obvious gully which has a chockstone in it (two cracks right of McCarthy North Face).

PITCH 1: Free climb the crack, up and over the bulge where a secure belay can be set (140 feet, 5.7). You could also traverse right one crack (5.9) and belay at a set of bolts. **PITCH 2:** Aid up the same crack until feasible to traverse left one crack (a hook move or a very long reach). Continue up the left hand crack to a small tree and a horizontal crack (120 feet, A2). A belay can be set here, or a better one can be found in the crack to the right. **PITCH 3:** Continue up the crack on tied-off knifeblades, thin pins, and even a RURP just under the small roof. Over the roof at the rope's end, the crack widens and allows an excellent belay on larger angles (160 feet, 5.7, A3+). **PITCH 4:** Climb up a few feet, then traverse left into the McCarthy North Face chimney (130 feet, 5.7). **FINISH:** Go to the top.

SUGGESTED EQUIPMENT: Standard aid rack and about 20 knifeblades, many tie-offs, 1 RURP, and a couple of hooks.

NOTE: This is one fine aid climb. It is composed of long pitches of thin nailing connected by wonderfully secure belays that come as knights in shining armor to your emotional rescue. Parts of this route have now been climbed free as Two Moons Over Hulett (Route 84).

83. GIMME SHELTER III, 5.7, A3 (Variation of Emotional Rescue)

FIRST ASCENT: May 29, 1981, solo by Frank Sanders. **APPROACH:** Same as Emotional Rescue (Route 82).

PITCH 1: Same as Emotional Rescue, Pitch 1 (140 feet, 5.7). **PITCH 2:** Aid up the same crack until feasible to traverse left. Gimme Shelter starts here and Emotional Rescue goes left. Aid up the same crack until level with a small tree on the left and a horizontal crack. The crux is a number of tied-off knifeblades. Set a belay here (120 feet, A3). **PITCH 3:** Lost Arrows and small angles lead ever upward. The aiding is easy and the view is just fine. Toward the end of the rope, as the crack withers, traverse left across the top of a small roof and belay on secure larger angles (160 feet, A1/A2). You are now back on Emotional Rescue. **PITCH 4:** Climb up a few feet, then traverse left into the McCarthy North Face chimney and follow that to the top (160 feet, 5.6). **FINISH:** Climb and scramble to the summit.

SUGGESTED EQUIPMENT: Standard aid rack and about a dozen knifeblades, 24 Lost Arrows, and some tie-offs.

NOTE: This is a highly enjoyable climb that is mostly secure nailing with a few thin spots for thrills.

84. TWO MOONS OVER HULETT II, 5.11b

FIRST ASCENT: July 24, 1983, by Dennis Horning and Dave Larsen. **APPROACH:** Same as Emotional Rescue (Route 82).

PITCH 1: Same as Emotional Rescue, Pitch 1. Traverse right one crack and belay at the bolts (150 feet, 5.9). **PITCH 2:** Climb up the crack a short distance and then step out onto the left face and climb on the crack and face holds there until you can traverse back to the same crack. Just above you on your right you will find two bolts to belay from (85 feet, 5.11b). **PITCH 3:** Climb the crack upward and onward to the next set of bolts on your right and set up your belay (85 feet, 5.10d). **PITCH 4:** Traverse left two columns and rejoin the old aid crack (Emotional Rescue) that you started out on. Climb up to the column top on your left where you take the left crack (McCarthy North Face, Route 80) and climb to the end of your rope. You should now be able to belay off a good ledge (160 feet, 5.7). **FINISH:** Continue up the crack to the summit (40 feet, 5.6).

SUGGESTED EQUIPMENT: Two sets of RPs, Rocks, and Friends to #3.

NOTE: You can also start this route on Klondike (Route 85), one crack right of the original start.

85. KLONDIKE I, 5.10a

FIRST ASCENT: August 15, 1983, by Dave Larsen and Dennis Horning. **APPROACH:** Take the Northeast Buttress Approach and traverse it west to the Northwest Shoulder just past McCarthy North Face (Route 80). This climb goes up below the face of Pitch 2 of Two Moons Over Hulett (Route 84) and is one crack right of Emotional Rescue (Route 82). Scramble up to a belay ledge 20 feet to the right of a large chockstone.

PITCH 1: Climb up the face through a five-foot-long, shallow dihedral. Continue up traversing right at a small roof, then continue up the face following the fixed protection to the belay bolts (150 feet, 5.10a). **FINISH:** Rappel from the bolts, or you can continue up on Two Moons Over Hulett or Emotional Rescue.

SUGGESTED EQUIPMENT: Quick draws, long runners, and small to medium Stoppers for use at start.

86. DR. ZEN III, 5.11c

FIRST ASCENT: As The Route of All Evil, July 24, 1969, by David Lunn, John Luz, and Bruce Morris (III, 5.8, A3). **FIRST FREE ASCENT:** September 1, 1983, by Steve Mankenberg and Dave Larsen. **APPROACH:** Go to the northwest corner of the Tower by the Northeast Buttress Approach or the West Face Approach. (Climbers use both.) The route lies between Klondike (Route 85) and Psychic Turbulence (Route 87) and follows the aid route The Route of All Evil.

PITCH 1: Two prominent roofs at the base of the climb help identify the start. Climb up to the left roof and pass it on its right. Continue up to the bolts for a belay where the two cracks separate from each other (130 feet, 5.8). **PITCH 2:** Climb the right crack straight up and belay at the bolts at a prominent outward-sloping edge (90 feet, 5.10). **PITCH 3:** Climb the crack and face above through three points of fixed protection. Traverse to the left crack and climb up to a stance where you can belay at the bolts (90 feet, 5.11c). **PITCH 4:** Climb the crack above until you come to a large ledge on your right where you can set up a belay (165 feet, 5.11a). **FINISH:** Scramble up to the summit (50 feet, 5.6).

SUGGESTED EQUIPMENT: Two sets of RPs, extra small and medium Stoppers, and #1 to #4 Friends.

87. PSYCHIC TURBULENCE I, 5.11a

FIRST ASCENT: August 15, 1984, by Todd Skinner, Daniel Rosen, and Beth Wald. **APPROACH:** This route is on the northwest corner and you can approach by the Northeast Buttress Approach or the West Face Approach. The route lies between Dr. Zen (Route 86) and Four Play (Route 88), two cracks right of Dr. Zen.

PITCH 1: Climb up just left of Four Play a short distance, traverse left under the crack, and set up a belay at the bolts (45 feet, 5.7). **PITCH 2:** This crack is a remarkable stemming pitch similar to El Matador (Route 121) but with thinner cracks and not as wide. Crank in an endurance factor for the calves. Use two ropes or have long runners. Protection can be placed in both cracks and as one crack runs out you can protect in the other. Two bolts in the middle are not crucial but are welcome (155 feet, 5.11a). **FINISH:** Rappel off or traverse right to Four Play and go to the summit on that.

SUGGESTED EQUIPMENT: Many small and medium RPs, two ropes or long runners, and a rack for the top pitches if you go to the summit.

88. FOUR PLAY III, 5.11c

FIRST ASCENT: May 25, 1980, by Steve Hong, Karin Budding, Mark Smedley, and Bill Feiges. **APPROACH:** Same as Northwest Corner (Route 89). Third or fourth class to the large flakes at a high stance at the start of Northwest Corner.

PITCH 1: Climb the left side of the flake and the thin finger crack above one crack left of Northwest Corner. Belay from bolts on the column top (160 feet, 5.11c). **PITCH 2:** Loose Flake. Climb the wide crack (right side) to a belay ledge (160 feet, 5.9). Several large Hexentrics protect this dirty pitch. **FINISH:** Climb easily straight up to the summit (20 feet, 5.4).

SUGGESTED EQUIPMENT: Three sets of medium RPs, three sets of small to medium Stoppers, two or three #1 Friends, and several large Hexentrics.

NOTE: On a scale of one to three, Steve Hong rates this a two-star climb.

89. NORTHWEST CORNER III, 5.8+, A3

FIRST ASCENT: July 16, 1961, by Layton Kor and Herb Swedlund. **APPROACH:** Take the West Face Approach and climb third class to the top of the Northwest Shoulder of the Tower. Belay from a small juniper tree. Looking up past the broken rock above you, you can see a small sloping ledge formed by the top of a broken column. The route runs up the crack on the right side of this column.

PITCH 1: Easy free climbing leads to a belay at the top of the broken section (150 feet, 5.5). **PITCH 2:** Climb straight up the small dirt- and moss-filled crack to a belay at a bolt (145 feet, A3). **PITCH 3:** Continue up on aid until it becomes possible to free climb to a belay at the top of a broken column on your left (80 feet, 5.6, A2). **PITCH 4:** Climb straight up the awkward chimney on the right, to a belay ledge at the top of the right-hand column (145 feet, 5.8+). **FINISH:** Climb cautiously over loose terrain up and left to the summit (45 feet, 5.5).

SUGGESTED EQUIPMENT: Large numbers of knifeblades and short, thick blades, and many hero loops. Four 1/2-inch angles, two 3/4-inch angles, two 1-inch angles, four #1 Stoppers, four #2 Stoppers, three #2-1/2 Stoppers, four #3 Stoppers, five #4 Stoppers, #6 to #9 Stoppers, #4 to #7 Hexentrics, three #11 Hexentrics, two 4-inch tube chocks, two 6-inch tube chocks, and gardening tools.

89
88
87
88
89
90

West Face

90. SPINEY NORMAN I, 5.12a

FIRST ASCENT: July 18, 1985, by Todd Skinner and Beth Wald. **APPROACH:** Take the West Face Approach or Northeast Buttress Approach until you are one crack right of Northwest Corner (Route 89) and one crack left of Carol's Crack (Route 91) where the route starts.

PITCH 1: Climb up this pitch which is basically a fingers and stemming problem. The crux is the last 10 feet. Set up a belay at the bolt and fixed nut (160 feet, 5.12a). **FINISH:** Rappel from here.

SUGGESTED EQUIPMENT: Many small wired Stoppers, two sets of medium to large RPs, and Friends up to #2.

NOTE: This is a two-star, fun pitch.

91. CAROL'S CRACK III, 5.11a

FIRST ASCENT: August 19, 1978, by Bob Yoho, Carol Black, Chick Holtkamp, and Jeff Baird. **APPROACH:** Take the West Face Approach and climb high on the Northwest Shoulder. This route is two cracks left of Approaching Lavender (Route 93).

PITCH 1: Begin at the large right-facing corner three cracks to the left of the start of One-Way Sunset (Route 94). Climb the corner, following the finger crack up to the double bolt belay at the foot hold on the right nose (100 feet, 5.10a). The crux is just below the bolts. **PITCH 2:** Follow the crack in the corner up to a hanging belay at the bolts (160 feet, 5.11a). This pitch is strenuous fingerlocks and stemming with few rests. **PITCH 3:** Follow the crack up to belay ledges on the right (60 feet, 5.7). **FINISH:** Climb the chimney above through a small roof and follow the crack to the summit (150 feet, 5.7).

SUGGESTED EQUIPMENT: Many medium wired Stoppers, around #7 and #8. Larger nuts are useful in the top two pitches (#8 to #10 Hexentrics).

NOTE: Most climbers rappel off at the top of Pitch 2.

92. RAINDANCE I, 5.10a

FIRST ASCENT: July 17, 1985, by Carl Coy and Beth Wald. **APPROACH:** Take the West Face or Northeast Buttress Approach and work over to the northwest corner of the Tower. Climb up to the base of Carol's Crack (Route 91). The route is one crack right of Carol's Crack.

PITCH 1: Follow the finger crack to a double bolt hanging belay (100 feet, 5.10a). The finger crack is initially straight in, then becomes shallow in an obtuse dihedral. Climbing is mostly fingertips and face moves, with a few flared hand jams. The crux is midway in the pitch, but the last couple of moves are also difficult. Protection is fair, and tricky to place. **FINISH:** Rappel from the bolts.

SUGGESTED EQUIPMENT: RPs, small to medium Stoppers, and Friends up to #2.

Opposite: North Face (left) and West Face

93. APPROACHING LAVENDER II, 5.11c

FIRST ASCENT: July 19, 1984, by Paul Piana, Bob Cowan, Todd Skinner, and Beth Wald. **APPROACH:** Take the West Face Approach and climb up to the base of Carol's Crack (Route 91), then traverse down and right to the start of One-Way Sunset (Route 94).

PITCH 1: Climb One-Way Sunset for about 40 feet (about 10 feet below the poor pitons). Traverse left to the route. The crack is the one that leads up to the left side of the two prominent roofs above you. It is also two cracks right of Carol's Crack. Stem and climb this crack about 100 feet to a hanging belay (140 feet, 5.11c). **PITCH 2:** Continue up with more painful stemming until you are below a roof. Step left to a stance and anchor at the bolts (80 feet, 5.11b). **FINISH:** Rappelling off from here is recommended, or you could continue up on some unaesthetic rubble.

SUGGESTED EQUIPMENT: Many small Stoppers, medium RPs, and a few mid-size Stoppers.

94. ONE-WAY SUNSET III, 5.10c

FIRST ASCENT: June 15, 1977, by Dennis Horning and Jim Slichter. **APPROACH:** Take the West Face Approach until you are directly below the double roofs on the north end of the West Face. This route starts in the crack that leads up between the two roofs. Climb to the base of Carol's Crack (Route 91) and traverse down and right to the start of the climb.

PITCH 1: Feather Fingers. Climb this thin crack 20 feet. Traverse right (5.9) to the crack on the face. Climb this crack (crux) with finger jams to the semihanging belay on a sloping ledge below a small roof (160 feet, 5.10c). **PITCH 2:** Climb this hand and fist crack through a roof to a good belay ledge with bolts (130 feet, 5.9). Sections of the crack are parallel sided and this crack is a rope eater, so use care pulling rappel ropes. **PITCH 3:** Degeneration. Continue up the line to a big belay ledge with bolts (70 feet, 5.9). **PITCH 4:** Overhanging. Climb the chimney crack to its end (80 feet, 5.8). A belay cave on the left offers a comfortable belay. **FINISH:** Escape. Traverse left from the belay cave to the obvious crack which leads to the summit (70 feet, 5.2).

SUGGESTED EQUIPMENT: Lots of #4 to #10 Stoppers, #5 to #11 Hexentrics, and a few large pieces.

NOTE: Most climbers only do the first two pitches and rappel.

95. BUSTER CATTLEFIELD I, 5.11d

FIRST ASCENT: September 3, 1985, by Tom Kalakay, Mal Ham, Bill Dockins, and Kristen Drumheller. **APPROACH:** Same as One-Way Sunset (Route 94). The pitch follows the start of One-Way Sunset but continues straight up the crack above the bent pins where One-Way Sunset traverses right one crack.

PITCH 1: Start on One-Way Sunset and continue up past the bent pins, where Buster Cattlefield starts. Climb up on stemming and good locks to a good hand jam. From here the difficulty goes up a grade. Climb the next 30 feet or so on very thin fingertip jamming and liebacking. This section protects well with RPs and #1 and #2 Rocks. Finish the pitch by traversing right to the One-Way Sunset

West Face

Pitch 1 belay stance (155 feet, 5.11d). **FINISH:** Rappel off or continue up on One-Way Sunset.

SUGGESTED EQUIPMENT: Many #2, #3 and #4 RPs; extra #1 and #2 Rocks, and #2, #2-1/2, and #3 Friends.

NOTE: This is an excellent thin-tip, liebacking pitch with good protection according to Tom Kalakay.

96. SYNCHRONICITY I, 5.11d

FIRST ASCENT: July 14, 1983, by Todd Skinner and John Rosholt. **APPROACH:** Same as One-Way Sunset (Route 94). Go right one crack to start the route.

PITCH 1: Belay at the headwall. Ascend into the right-facing corner (crux). Continue up the crack to a semihanging belay (130 feet, 5.10). **PITCH 2:** Move up on desperate, endurance stemming. Two ropes are helpful as you need to protect in two separate cracks; or bring long runners. Continue up until the crack opens enough to accept good Friends and Stoppers. Set up a hanging belay here (130 feet, 5.11d). **PITCH 3:** Continue stemming up the same crack system until the left crack turns left and joins the top of Pitch 2 of One-Way Sunset (120 feet, 5.10c). **FINISH:** It would be possible to continue in dirty dihedrals to the summit. You may want to rappel off or go to the summit via One-Way Sunset.

SUGGESTED EQUIPMENT: A set of Stoppers and a set of Friends.

NOTE: According to Todd Skinner, this route makes El Matador (Route 121) look like an off width!

97. DELI EXPRESS II, 5.12a

FIRST ASCENT: June 26, 1983, by Mark Sonnenfeld and Steve Hong. **APPROACH:** Take the West Face Approach until you are just left of center of the West Face. This crack is seven cracks right of One-Way Sunset at its midpoint.

PITCH 1: Climb up easy bulges to a belay pod below the steep section (30 feet, 5.7). **PITCH 2:** Climb this long and increasingly difficult crack to one bolt on your right at a foot-hold hanging belay stance (165 feet, 5.11d). **PITCH 3:** Continue up the crack to a two-bolt stance (90 feet, 5.12a). **FINISH:** Rappel off — top rotten section is totally mungy.

SUGGESTED EQUIPMENT: Two to four sets of RPs, over 30 carabiners, two #1 and two #2 Friends, and 25 assorted small nuts.

98. VERROUILLER LETOIT PENDANG LA MARCHE II, 5.7, A3

FIRST ASCENT: July 30, 1985, by Kyle Copeland and John Gill. **APPROACH:** Take the West Face Approach. The climb is in the first corner left of No Holds for Bonzo (Route 101), the NAM Column.

PITCH 1: Moderate free climbing (5.7) leads to the start of the aid climbing. Continue up on aid to a hanging belay from three bolts (130 feet, 5.7, A3). The crux is encountered approximately 30 feet below the belay. **PITCH 2:** Climb up on aid in this thin crack through the crux about 20 feet up. Continue up past a set of double bolts, using thin pins to the end of the pitch which has only two knifeblades and a sling to belay/rappel from (125 feet, A3). Set your own protection here. **FINISH:** Rappel from here.

SUGGESTED EQUIPMENT: Forty bugaboos and knifeblades, five Lost Arrows, a #1 Friend, two sets of RPs, a #9 Stopper, and a selection of small wires. Take lots of hero loops and about fifty carabiners.

NOTE: Falcon attacks limited the upward progress so bolts could not be placed at the end. The second ascent party needs to place bolts to rappel from.

99. NAM I, 5.8

FIRST ASCENT: July 7, 1985, by Dick Guilmette and Bruce Adams. **APPROACH:** Follow the West Face Approach until you are between Saber (Route 103) and Deli Express (Route 97). This is about four cracks left of Saber. The crack goes up the left side of the prominent NAM Column, which looks like a knife sliced off a piece at a steep angle. Belay low in a left-facing corner with a small tree on your right.

PITCH 1: Climb up on friction about 45 feet to the crux of the pitch. This awkward bulge can be climbed by stepping up left and twisting to the right and up on awkward moves. Easy climbing brings you to the belay under an overhang (90 feet, 5.8). **FINISH:** Rappel from here on your own placements, or climb the next pitch, which has now gone free as No Holds for Bonzo, Route 101 (110 feet, 5.11b).

SUGGESTED EQUIPMENT: Small to medium Stoppers. If you plan to do the second pitch (originally aided), see No Holds for Bonzo for equipment to free climb it.

100. RISQUE I, 5.12

FIRST ASCENT: August 10, 1985, by Todd Skinner, Beth Wald, Jim Schlinkmann, and Bill Hatcher. **APPROACH:** Take the West Face Approach to the base of the NAM Column. The route is the arête on the left side of No Holds for Bonzo (Route 101). Belay high in a cleft (NAM) 15 feet below the first bolt. You will be just above and left of a lone tree.

PITCH 1: Follow the sharp arête past seven protection bolts, using everything except the dihedral. Set up a hanging belay at the double bolts (80 feet, 5.12). **FINISH:** Rappel down.

SUGGESTED EQUIPMENT: Seven quick draws and a level head.

NOTE: According to Todd Skinner this is a three-star classic pitch that is unique to the Tower.

101. NO HOLDS FOR BONZO I, 5.11b

FIRST ASCENT: July 16, 1985, by Mateo Pee Pee and Jim Schlinkmann. **APPROACH:** Same as NAM (Route 99). This route follows the original aid route.

PITCH 1: Same as NAM (5.8), or a fourth-class climb above a pine tree angling up and left (90 feet, 5.8). **PITCH 2:** Surmount the overhang and follow the left-facing corner to a small belay ledge with bolts (110 feet, 5.11b). The climbing is sustained, with stemming, face climbing, and great fingerlocks. The crux is a thin section 15 feet from the end of the pitch. **FINISH:** Rappel from bolts.

SUGGESTED EQUIPMENT: Many small to medium Stoppers, RPs, and at least one medium Hexentric or #2 Friend for flake midway in pitch.

NOTE: Belay 20 feet below the overhang in order to watch the leader above. This climb has excellent protection and is destined to become a one-pitch West Face classic. It gets three stars.

102. POTATOES ALIEN I, 5.10b

FIRST ASCENT: July 10, 1985, by Mateo Pee Pee, Steve "Barney" Fisher, and Jim Schlinkmann. **APPROACH:** Take the West Face Approach. The route follows the right edge of the NAM Column. It is just right of NAM and No Holds for Bonzo (Route 101). Begin the route below a four-foot flake slightly to the right of the upper crack that marks the right side of the column.

PITCH 1: Climb the flake, then move slightly up and left to a bulge which is surmounted directly using face holds (5.8). Follow the curving crack above first to the right and then to the left. Belay on a superb ledge using nut anchors (110 feet, 5.8). **PITCH 2:** Follow the crack above for approximately 20 feet, then traverse left onto a large ledge. A couple of face moves lead back right to the thin crack that leads to the top of the column. Belay at the bolts (60 feet, 5.10b). **FINISH:** Rappel from the bolts.

SUGGESTED EQUIPMENT: Small to medium Stoppers, one to five Rocks, RPs, and a #1 Friend.

NOTE: This climb gets one to two stars; three is the best.

103. SABER IV, 5.6, A3

FIRST ASCENT: April 26, 1964, by Layton Kor and Floyd Tex Bossier. **APPROACH:** Looking at the West Face of the Tower from the Visitor Center you will see a dark crack running diagonally up from right to left in the top, rough portion of the Tower. This is located almost in the center of the West Face. Just below the bottom of this crack is a small roof. The route begins at the top of the shoulder, in the crack that runs up to the left side of this roof. Climb up the West Face Approach and work your way up to the start of the route. This is two cracks left of Brokedown Palace (Route 107) which is the free ascent of the old aid crack Conquest of Tillie's Lookout. It is also one crack left of Bloodguard (Route 105). Belay high.

PITCH 1: Same as Spank the Monkey, Route 104 (140 feet, 5.11a). **PITCH 2:** Continue up the crack on aid, setting up a hanging belay a few feet below the roof (120 feet, A2). **PITCH 3:** Continue up on aid and pass the roof on the left. Use aid up this crack until it becomes possible to free climb to a third hanging belay (150 feet, 5.6, A3). **FINISH:** Free climb the large diagonal crack on your left until it becomes possible to scramble to the summit (75 feet, 5.6).

SUGGESTED EQUIPMENT: A generous selection of pins, including many blades and several bongs for protection on the upper portions. Nuts may work well on the upper half of this route and may help eliminate the need to clean pigeon dung from the crack.

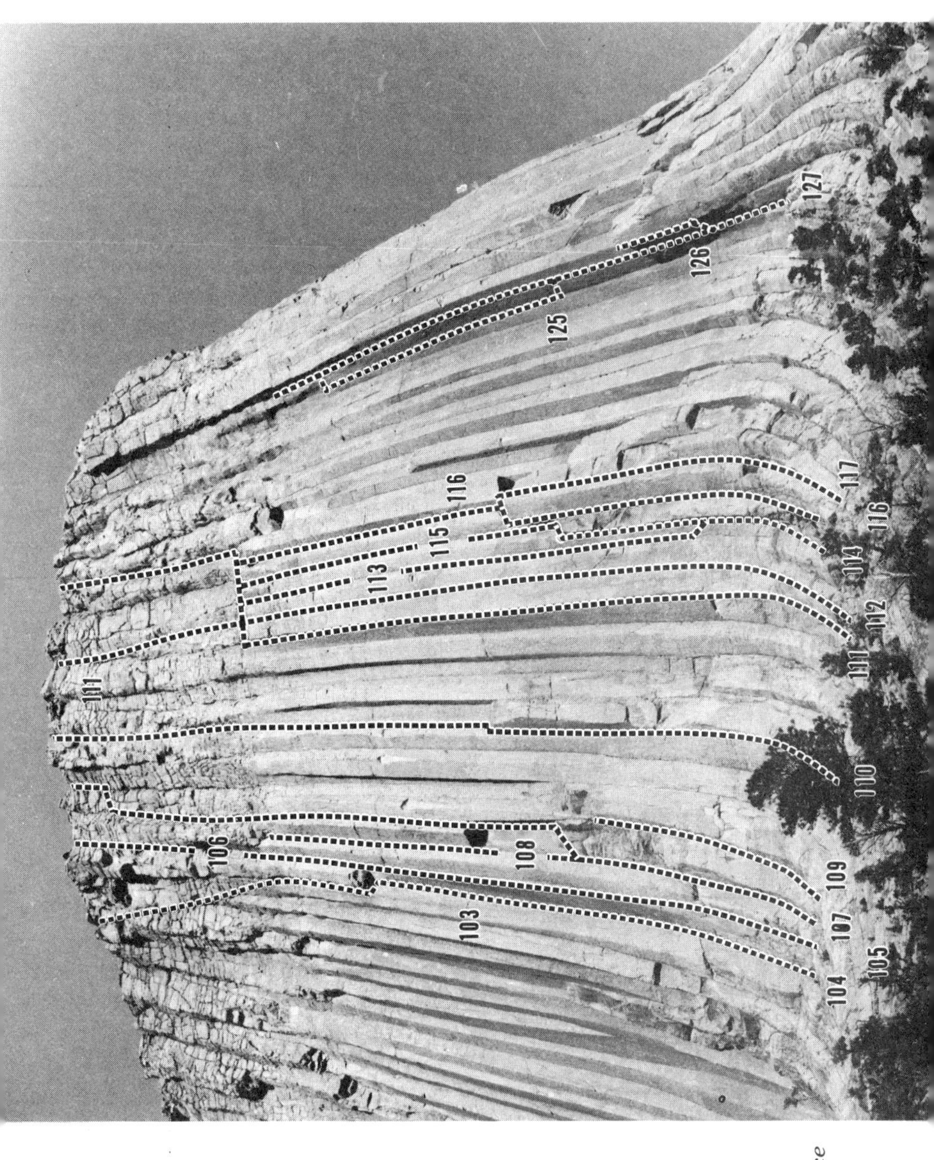

101
106
103
108
110
111
112
113
114
115
116
116
117
125
126
127
104
105
107
109

West Face

104. SPANK THE MONKEY I, 5.11a

FIRST ASCENT: As Saber, April 26, 1964, by Layton Kor and Tex Bossier (IV, 5.6, A3). **FIRST FREE ASCENT:** August 22, 1985, by Jim Schlinkmann, Mateo Pee Pee, and Carl Coy (first pitch only). **APPROACH:** Take the West Face Approach until you are left of Brokedown Palace (Route 107). The climb follows the first pitch of the aid route Saber (Route 103) and is one crack left of Bloodguard (Route 105).

PITCH 1: Climb the dihedral to a double bolt hanging belay (140 feet, 5.11a). The lower half of the climb is a tricky 5.8+ hand crack. The remaining 80 feet follows a beautiful dihedral and utilizes intermittent cracks on the right face. Climbing involves fingerlocks, face moves, and strenuous stemming. The crux is cranking on fingertips off a good rest ledge, about 20 feet below the bolts. Good rests and excellent protection. **FINISH:** Rappel from bolts.

SUGGESTED EQUIPMENT: #3 and #3-1/2 Friends for lower hand crack; two full sets of Rocks and RPs, plus Sliders helpful.

NOTE: This is destined to become another short West Face classic, similar in flavor to No Holds for Bonzo (Route 101).

105. BLOODGUARD I, 5.12a

FIRST ASCENT: As Non-Dairy Creamer, October 12, 1977, by Chris Ballinger, Jim Lynch, and Frank Sanders (III, 5.8, A3). **FIRST FREE ASCENT:** July 19, 1984, by Todd Skinner, Beth Wald, Bob Cowan, and Paul Piana. **APPROACH:** Same as Non-Dairy Creamer (Route 106). This route is between Spank the Monkey (Route 104) and Brokedown Palace (Route 107).

PITCH 1: This is an amazing, straight-in finger crack with perfect protection and several hands-down rests. It is exhilarating and exposed with the crux at the end (160 feet, 5.12a). Very thin, steep tip jamming on the last 20 feet adds a full grade to the pitch. **FINISH:** Rappel or climb Non-Dairy Creamer to the summit.

SUGGESTED EQUIPMENT: Many medium Stoppers on the first 140 feet and several RPs on the last 20 feet.

NOTE: Any parties wishing to aid this, please use nuts so as not to destroy the superb free climbing. Todd Skinner says this is a three-star route.

106. NON-DAIRY CREAMER III, 5.12a, A3

FIRST ASCENT: October 12, 1977, by Chris Ballinger, Jim Lynch, and Frank Sanders. **APPROACH:** Same as Saber (Route 103). The route starts one crack right of Saber and one crack left of Brokedown Palace (Route 107). Belay high.

PITCH 1: Same as Bloodguard, Route 105 (160 feet, 5.12a). **PITCH 2:** Continue up the crack on aid, setting up a hanging belay a few feet below the roof (110 feet, A2). **PITCH 3:** Climb to the roof and pass it on the right. Continue up on aid until you have to hang a belay near the end of your rope (155 feet, A3). **FINISH:** Continue up the same crack to the summit.

SUGGESTED EQUIPMENT: No list was given by first-ascent climbers.

107. BROKEDOWN PALACE III, 5.12a

FIRST ASCENT: As Conquest of Tillie's Lookout, August 10, 1973, by Bruce Price and Mike LaLone (III, 5.8, A2). **FIRST FREE ASCENT:** October 2, 1981, by Steve Hong and Mark Sonnenfeld. **APPROACH:** Take the West Face Approach past Vulture (Route 110) until you are below a prominent roof in the middle of the West Face. The crack is below the left side of the overhang and one crack right of Bloodguard (Route 105).

PITCH 1: Climb the left crack leading to a small belay ledge below the roof. Protection is difficult. Belay at double corner bolts (160 feet, 5.11a). **PITCH 2:** Climb the right crack and out the right lip of the roof and up the crack 20 feet to small foot holds for a hanging belay at a bolt and fixed pin (70 feet, 5.12a). **PITCH 3:** Climb the finger crack above to the base of the exit chimney and an awkward belay (130 feet, 5.11c). **FINISH:** Climb the grotesque chimney above about 100 feet to a bolt under the crux bulge. Traverse right here and continue up somewhat easier climbing to the summit (130 feet, 5.7). This pitch has marginal protection and very loose rock.

SUGGESTED EQUIPMENT: Three sets of medium RPs, numerous #4 to #8 Stoppers, #1 Friends, and perhaps large sliders (25 pieces altogether).

NOTE: Steve Hong considers this a three-star classic route but recommends rappelling after Pitch 3.

108. AVALON II, 5.11d

FIRST ASCENT: July 26, 1984, by Todd Skinner and Beth Wald. **APPROACH:** Exactly the same as Brokedown Palace (Route 107).

PITCH 1: Same as Brokedown Palace, Pitch 1, to a belay ledge and bolts (160 feet, 5.11a). **PITCH 2:** Take the left crack off the ledge, using very thin fingerlocks and stemming to small edges to reach a stance underneath the roof. Make a classic 5.10 move to pull the roof and continue up a beautiful finger crack to a hanging belay on pins and a fixed nut (80 feet, 5.11d). **PITCH 3:** Continue the wild finger crack, which becomes significantly harder (involving continuously desperate stemming and thin fingers with a few rests) to a welcome ledge. Belay on fixed pins (100 feet, 5.11c). **FINISH:** Rappel from here or face the wrath of loose, filthy boulders.

SUGGESTED EQUIPMENT: Many RPs and small to medium Stoppers.

NOTE: Todd Skinner gives this route a three-star rating.

109. JERRY'S KIDS I, 5.10b

FIRST ASCENT: July 21, 1985, by Jim Schlinkmann, Mateo Pee Pee, and "Barney" Fisher. **APPROACH:** Same as Brokedown Palace (Route 107). The route follows the crack right of Pitch 1 of Brokedown Palace (West Face Approach).

PITCH 1: Follow the crack in the left-facing corner to a comfortable belay ledge with bolts (120 feet, 5.10b). Climbing involves fingertips, face moves, and stemming. The crux is a continuous thin section for 20 feet above the second bolt in the lower half of the pitch, until you reach a bomber #2-1/2 Friend placement.

Three bolts help protect this pitch. Overall protection is good but strenuous to place. Good rests. **FINISH:** Rappel from bolts.

SUGGESTED EQUIPMENT: Wired Stoppers, two sets of RPs, #1-1/2 and #2-1/2 Friends, sliders, and quick draws.

NOTE: Belay comfortably at the juniper tree at the base of the route.

110. VULTURE IV, 5.12a, A3

FIRST ASCENT: May 13, 1961, by Layton Kor and Bob LaGrange (IV, 5.8, A3). Finish variation to West Face Ledge June 28, 1976, by Glen Banks and Paul Horak. **FIRST FREE ASCENT:** of the first two pitches — July 9, 1985, by Steve Hong, Karin Budding, and Beth Wald. **APPROACH:** Take the West Face Approach to the center of the West Face. This route follows the crack up the left side of a column that ends halfway up the center of the West Face. This is midway between Brokedown Palace (Route 107) and Mr. Clean (Route 111).

PITCH 1: Climb up the left side of the Vulture Pillar, an insipient crack and face climb. Set up a belay at a stance (50 feet, 5.7). Protection is poor. **PITCH 2:** Continue up the crack with fingerlocks, face moves, and liebacking to the comfortable ledge on top of the Vulture Pillar (165 feet, 5.12a). The crux is a short distance below the top. Protection is poor at the start. **PITCH 3:** Sustained difficult aid for about 100 feet leads to a not-so-reassuring belay from tied-off pins in a horizontal crack (100 feet, A3). This pitch takes lots of tied-off knifeblades, and Crack-n-ups help considerably. **PITCH 4:** Continue up shaky aid about 70 feet to where it becomes possible to climb free. Kor went straight up to very poor rock. It is best to traverse right (free) at this point, several columns, and belay at the West Face Ledge (90 feet, 5.8, A3). **FINISH:** Climb straight up Mr. Clean to the summit (160 feet, 5.8). There is loose rock and poor protection.

SUGGESTED EQUIPMENT (for Pitches 1 and 2 free): Three sets each RPs and #1, #2, and #4 Rocks. One set medium Stoppers, two #2-1/2 Friends for first belay, and two #1, #2, and #1-1/2 Friends. Equipment for aid: #1 to #9 Hexentrics, #1 to #4 wired Stoppers, #1 to #4 Copperheads, #1 to #4 Crack-n-ups, and assorted pitons from knifeblades to a 3/4-inch angle.

111. MR. CLEAN III, 5.11a

FIRST ASCENT: July 30, 1976, by Curt Haire and Dennis Horning (III, 5.10, A1). **FIRST FREE ASCENT:** August 14, 1977, by Henry Barber and Chip Lee. **APPROACH:** Use the West Face Approach. The line follows the crack just left of Misty Morning Melody (Route 112) and halfway between Vulture (Route 110) and Tulgey Wood (Route 116). Begin the route below a bright yellow one-foot-wide roof at a bolt. You may want to fourth class the 30 feet (5.6) up to the bolt.

PITCH 1: Climb up through the roof (5.10d) and the long finger crack above it until you get to the belay bolts on your left (160 feet, 5.11a). This is strenuous with the only true rest halfway up, a small ledge on the right face. **PITCH 2:** Continue up the same line with hand and fist jams to the West Face Ledge (160 feet, 5.10a). **FINISH:** Move one column right and follow the large crack to the summit (160 feet, 5.9).

SUGGESTED EQUIPMENT: #1 to #8 Hexentrics, #3 to #12 Stoppers with many extra #7 to #10s. Friends are helpful.

112. MISTY MORNING MELODY II, 5.8, A2

FIRST ASCENT: June 1, 1980, by Steve Gardiner, Frank Sanders, and Mark Brackin. **APPROACH:** Use the Durrance Approach to the top of the boulder field below McCarthy West Face (Route 118). Climb up to the base of the route which lies one crack right of Mr. Clean (Route 111).

PITCH 1: Climb up the crack on aid to a hanging belay at a point where the crack widens slightly (150 feet, A2). **PITCH 2:** Continue on aid until you run out of rope and hopefully reach the West Face Ledge (165 feet, A2). **FINISH:** Traverse to the right and finish the climb free, using the last two pitches of McCarthy West Face to the summit (100 feet, 5.8 and 70 feet, 5.5).

SUGGESTED EQUIPMENT: Full rack of Stoppers and Hexentrics plus a good selection of knifeblades, Lost Arrows, and angles.

113. INDEPENDENCE III, 5.8, A3

FIRST ASCENT: July 4, 1980, solo by Frank Sanders. **APPROACH:** Same as Tulgey Wood (Route 116). This route is one crack left of Tulgey Wood.

PITCH 1: Work your way up this crack until it is feasible to move left one crack just over halfway up the Tulgey Wood Column. Continue up until you are out of rope and set up a hanging belay (160 feet, A2). **PITCH 2:** Stay in the same crack and aid up to the end of your rope and hang a belay (155 feet, A2). **PITCH 3:** More of the same except the last 20 feet to the West Face Ledge, which is hard to figure out. Belay here (60 feet, A3). **FINISH:** Rappel down or climb to the summit on McCarthy West Face, Route 118 (100 feet, 5.8).

SUGGESTED EQUIPMENT: Lots of knifeblades, bugaboos, and Lost Arrows.

NOTE: Hanging belays are quite secure. The first portion of Pitch 1 has been climbed free as A Bridge Too Far (Route 114).

114. A BRIDGE TOO FAR I, 5.11d

FIRST ASCENT: June 27, 1983, by Todd Skinner, Mark Sonnenfeld, and Steve Hong. **APPROACH:** Same as Tulgey Wood (Route 116) and McCarthy West Face (Route 118). The two cracks used are one and two cracks left of Tulgey Wood and stemming between them. "It is impossible for people under five-foot six," says Steve Hong.

PITCH 1: This is in the first corner left of Tulgey Wood. Work up until you can stem one crack left. Climb on desperate stemming past a bolt to Tulgey Wood's first belay on a column top (140 feet, 5.11d). **FINISH:** Rappel down or continue to the summit on other routes.

SUGGESTED EQUIPMENT: Double 9mm rope recommended because you need to protect in both cracks; or bring runners if you're poor. Two sets of RPs and #6 to #8 Stoppers for the upper portion of the pitch.

NOTE: Steve Hong rates this a one-star route on a scale of one to three.

115. ADVENTUROUS DAZE IV, 5.10a, A2 or A3

FIRST ASCENT: June 4, 1983, by Frank Sanders and Chris Engle. **APPROACH:** Same as Tulgey Wood (Route 116) or A Bridge Too Far (Route 114).

PITCH 1: Take A Bridge Too Far (140 feet, 5.11d) or Tulgey Wood, Pitch 1 (130 feet, 5.10a), which is easier. **PITCH 2:** Aid up the left crack from the first belay ledge of Tulgey Wood, then hang a belay (160 feet, A2 to A3). **PITCH 3:** Continue on aid up the same crack until you reach the West Face Meadows (60 feet, A2). **FINISH:** Climb on McCarthy West Face (Route 118) to the summit.

SUGGESTED EQUIPMENT: Aid cracks need a standard aid rack and a wide assortment of Lost Arrows and knifeblades. Also take small to medium pieces for the free portion of the climb and a few larger pieces for the top.

116. TULGEY WOOD III, 5.10a

FIRST ASCENT: June 2, 1972, by Mark Hesse and Dan McClure. **APPROACH:** Take the Durrance Approach to the tower base and angle up left until you are just north of the McCarthy West Face roof (Route 118). The climb is one crack left of Way Layed (Route 117) in the obvious left-facing dihedral.

PITCH 1: Climb this hand and finger crack to the column top bolts on your left (130 feet, 5.10a). **PITCH 2:** Climb the finger crack and stem to the column top bolts on your right (30 feet, 5.10a). **PITCH 3:** Climb the long fist crack to a large ledge (West Face Ledge) (160 feet, 5.9). **FINISH:** Take the McCarthy West Face route to the summit (160 feet, 5.8).

SUGGESTED EQUIPMENT: Full rack plus extra small to medium Stoppers and about five 2- to 3-1/4-inch pieces. #4 Friends help on Pitch 3.

117. WAY LAYED I, 5.11b

FIRST ASCENT: June 30, 1981, by Eric Rhicard and Mark Smedley. **APPROACH:** Same as McCarthy West Face (Route 118). This climb is in the crack that runs up to the left side of the prominent McCarthy West Face roof.

PITCH 1: Climb the right-facing corner crack to the top of Tulgey Wood Column (155 feet, 5.11b). This crack is sustained thin fingers and stemming, with the crux at the roof. **FINISH:** Rappel from here or continue on Tulgey Wood (Route 116) to the summit.

SUGGESTED EQUIPMENT: Small Stoppers, Friends, and RPs.

118. McCARTHY WEST FACE III, 5.11c

FIRST ASCENT: July 26, 1955, by James McCarthy and John Rupley (5.8, A3). This was the first route established on the West Face. **FIRST FREE ASCENT:** August 11, 1979, by Steve Hong and Karin Budding. **APPROACH:** Take the Durrance Approach to the West Face. Climb up and slightly left until you are below the prominent gray roofs. This route is two cracks right of Tulgey Wood (Route 116) and one crack left of El Matador (Route 121).

PITCH 1: Belay from the ledge below the first bulge. The crux is 15 feet above here. Climb the left crack to the top of a column that forms a large, prominent flake (110 feet, 5.9). **PITCH 2:** From the belay, climb the rightmost of the three cracks to belay on top of the right column (95 feet, 5.11c). **PITCH 3:** Hand jam to a ledge directly below the ceilings (60 feet, 5.8). **PITCH 4:** This pitch can be done two ways: immediately traverse left from the ledge and fist jam the crack, turning roofs on the left; or climb directly up the center crack to a fixed pin and hand traverse left, also turning ceilings on left. Belay on the West Face Ledge (65 feet, 5.7). **PITCH 5:** Climb the rightmost crack through two overhanging squeeze chimneys, the second of which is the crux of the pitch. Belay on a broad ledge directly after the last overhang (100 feet, 5.8). **FINISH:** Climb the crack to the summit, traversing slightly left (70 feet, 5.5).

SUGGESTED EQUIPMENT: Full set of Hexentrics and Stoppers with extra #5 to #12 Stoppers and runners. A 4-inch piece is helpful on Pitch 5.

NOTE: You can reach the top of Pitch 2 of Tulgey Wood by climbing up and left from the top of Pitch 1 of McCarthy West Face. This small traverse was first done July 7, 1976, by Greg Newth and Dave Hoag and is called the McCarthy West Face Heads Up Variation. You can rappel from here, as some do, or continue up on Tulgey Wood (30 feet, 5.10a).

119. McCARTHY WEST FACE—FREE VARIATION II, 5.10b

FIRST ASCENT: July 1, 1978, by Chris Ballinger, Dennis Horning, and Steve Gardiner. **APPROACH:** Same as McCarthy West Face (Route 118).

PITCH 1: Same as McCarthy West Face, Pitch 1 (110 feet, 5.9). **PITCH 2:** Climb the left crack (McCarthy West Face — Heads Up Variation halfway). Climb up and pass the roof on the right, using a finger crack. Avoid rope drag under the roof and use wide stemming to reach the top of Pitch 3 of McCarthy West Face (155 feet, 5.10b). **PITCH 3:** Same as El Matador (Route 121), Pitch 1 — up and right through the gray roofs (160 feet, 5.10a). **FINISH:** Continue to the summit (60 feet, 5.4).

SUGGESTED EQUIPMENT: A full rack of Stoppers and Hexentrics with extra medium and large Stoppers.

120. McCARTHY WEST FACE—HONG VARIATION I, 5.11c

FIRST ASCENT: May 11, 1979, by Steve Hong and Karin Budding. **APPROACH:** Same as McCarthy West Face (Route 118).

PITCH 1: Start at the base of the McCarthy West Face crack and climb the crack up under the overhang and pass it on the right, which is the crux. Continue up the thin crack with fingerlocks to a belay at the bolts above the flake (130 feet, 5.11c). **FINISH:** Rappel off or go to the summit via any of the routes above.

SUGGESTED EQUIPMENT: For Hong Variation, many RPs and small wired Stoppers.

NOTE: This is Grade III if you go to the summit. Steve Hong rates it a 5.11b, while others call it 5.11c.

121. EL MATADOR III, 5.10d

FIRST ASCENT: September 24, 1967, by Fred Beckey and Eric Bjornstad (IV, 5.7, A3). **FIRST FREE ASCENT:** August 6, 1978, by Bob Yoho and Chick Holtkamp.

118
124
130
118
123
121
129
118
116
119
123
128
130
126
120
130
131
129
117
118
121
122
124

West Face

APPROACH: This route leaves the shoulder of the Tower two cracks to the right of McCarthy West Face (Route 118).

PITCH 1: Follow the right hand crack up to the obvious belay at the two bolts below the chimney (80 feet, 5.8+). The crux is a finger crack in the last 15 feet. **PITCH 2:** Stem the chimney and jam the left crack, fingers and hand, to the top of the column (130 feet, 5.10d). This pitch is continuous 5.9. Obviously a height-dependent pitch — harder for short people. **PITCH 3:** Same as McCarthy West Face, Pitch 3 (60 feet, 5.8). **PITCH 4:** Climb the left hand crack to a fixed pin. Then traverse into the right hand crack by a second fixed pin. Climb the finger crack through this roof (crux) to a second roof, and through that one continue up the 5.7 chimney on good holds. Continue up a larger finger crack (5.9) to a stance with a bolt (160 feet, 5.10a). **FINISH:** Climb the chimney to the summit (60 feet, 5.4).

SUGGESTED EQUIPMENT: #3 to #8 Hexentrics, #1 to #3 Friends, runners for overhangs, and a full set of Stoppers. Also, extra small Stoppers and long slings to prevent rope drag over gray roofs.

NOTE: Most people rappel off from Pitch 2. If you do this, *be sure* to rappel *down the face* (not the crack) to prevent jamming your ropes.

122. DIGITAL EXTRACTION III, 5.11d

FIRST ASCENT: October 25, 1977, by Keith Lober, as Made for Aid (III, 5.8, A3). **FIRST FREE ASCENT:** May 19, 1982, by Steve Hong and Mark Sonnenfeld. **APPROACH:** Take the Durrance Approach until you reach the solid rock. Scramble mostly up and slightly left until you are just right of the start of El Matador. The climb follows the first crack right of the El Matador box, except for the first few feet, where it is two cracks right.

PITCH 1: Climb this severe, thin crack until you can set up a hanging belay at a bolt (110 feet, 5.11c). **PITCH 2:** This pitch is continuously sustained with thin jamming at the crux near the end of the pitch and the end of your strength. There are fixed pins at the hanging belay (140 feet, 5.11d). **PITCH 3:** Rappel (recommended) or climb up the crack until you can belay from two bolts on your right. Crux in mid-point (100 feet, 5.10). **FINISH:** Climb the final chimney above to the summit (130 feet, 5.8).

SUGGESTED EQUIPMENT: Take three to four sets of large RPs and a double set of #3 to #7 Stoppers. Also #1 to #4 Friends or Hexentrics, three #1 and two #3 Friends for the first two pitches. Take larger nuts for the upper pitches.

NOTE: If you rappel off, it is only Grade II. Steve Hong rates this a three star route on a scale of one to three stars.

123. THE THIN DAGGER IV, A2

FIRST ASCENT: September 13, 1980, by Dan Grady and Rod Johnson. **APPROACH:** Follow the Durrance Approach until you are halfway up to the top of the Southwest Shoulder. From here you need to work your way up and just left of the Southwest Buttress onto a large belay ledge. This route starts about two cracks left of the large, left-facing dihedral on your right. This crack leads to The Thin Dagger (Route 123) farther up. Looking up you will see a fairly uniform, continuous crack that starts in a small, right-facing dihedral, stays there for a few feet, and higher up runs up the edge of the large, left-facing dihedral on your right. This is the route.

CLIMB: Aid up the Conquistador crack until you come to the point of The Thin Dagger, which is about 110 feet up. Take the left side. The entire crack is a thin knifeblade-to-Lost-Arrow crack with an occasional baby angle or # 1 or # 2 wired Stopper. It continues for about 380 feet straight up with hanging belays. **FINISH:** Traverse left to a pitch of easy free climbing to the summit.

SUGGESTED EQUIPMENT: Plenty of blades and Lost Arrows, with some small angles and wired Stoppers.

NOTE: These two routes have been climbed only once. The first-ascent climbers submitted their reports in the form included here. Since details about belay locations and crux information is vague, anyone wishing to climb either of these routes should take extra caution.

124. CONQUISTADOR IV, 5.7, A3

FIRST ASCENT: May 3, 1964, by Floyd Tex Bossier and Steve Komito. **APPROACH:** Exactly the same as the approach to The Thin Dagger (Route 123).

CLIMB: Aid up this thin crack about 110 feet, where you will see The Thin Dagger crack angling up to the left. Continue straight up to a hanging belay at the end of your rope. Continue up the same crack until you reach the weathered portion, about 170 feet below the summit. At this point traverse one crack left and climb up to an overhang. **FINISH:** Traverse left one crack and climb to the summit (5.7, A3).

SUGGESTED EQUIPMENT: A large selection of blades and tie-offs, a standard selection of angles, and a few bongs for protection on the upper portions of the climb. Nuts can also be used.

NOTE: These two routes have been climbed only once. The first-ascent climbers submitted their reports in the form included here. Since details about belay locations and crux information is vague, anyone wishing to climb either of these routes should take extra caution.

125. WHITE LIGHTNING III, A2

FIRST ASCENT: September 1, 1985, by Mark Gordon and Kristi Rolf. **APPROACH:** Same as Conquistador (Route 124) or Abject Cathexis (Route 126). The pitch is between Conquistador and Abject Cathexis. To reach it you have to start in Abject Cathexis.

PITCH 1: Same as Abject Cathexis, Pitch 1 (140 feet, A2). **PITCH 2:** White Lightning. Pendulum one crack to the left. Aid up this crack on knifeblades (crux) about 35 feet to where the crack opens up to small Stoppers and Lost Arrows. Continue aiding up this crack about 110 feet to where you can see a bucket hold off to your right. Tension traverse back to Abject Cathexis one crack right. Aid this crack about 15 feet to the fixed pins hanging belay (160 feet, A2). This is at the base of the broken section of the Tower rock. **FINISH:** Rappel off down to the anchors (fixed pins) on The Thin Dagger (Route 123) and down to the starting ledge from there. Due to the overhanging nature of the dihedral, you cannot rappel directly down the route you went up on.

SUGGESTED EQUIPMENT: Many #1 to #5 Stoppers and some larger ones; steel nuts, knifeblades, and Lost Arrows.

NOTE: One could swing out of Abject Cathexis into the left hand crack sooner, but this would definitely increase the difficulty. This climb is a gas! The pendulum and the tension traverse are great.

126. ABJECT CATHEXIS III, A3

FIRST ASCENT: May 27, 1983, by Eric Breitenberger and William Trull. **APPROACH:** Take the Durrance Approach onto the Tower base and then straight up to the high ledge that starts Conquistador (Route 124). You are also just left of the Southwest Buttress. The route is in the second main crack right of Conquistador. This is the outermost crack in the left-facing dihedral between Conquistador and the Southwest Buttress.

PITCH 1: Aid up this dihedral. At the end of your rope set up a belay on nuts or pins (140 feet, A2). **PITCH 2:** Continue aiding up the same crack in the overhanging dihedral until you reach the broken rock. The crux is just below the end. Set up a hanging belay at the fixed pins (140 feet, A3). **FINISH:** Rappel off or continue up on Conquistador or The Thin Dagger (Route 123) to the summit.

SUGGESTED EQUIPMENT: Nuts up to #8, #1 to #1-1/2 Friends, and lots of RPs, especially #5.

NOTE: This is rated a very good aid climb.

127. BILLIE BEAR CRANKS THE RAD I, 5.12a

FIRST ASCENT: August 12, 1985, by Bill Hatcher, Todd Skinner, and Rick Erker. **APPROACH:** Take the Durrance Approach onto the lower shoulder, then straight up to a large ledge at the base of Conquistador (Route 124). The route follows the start of Abject Cathexis (Route 126), then traverses right into the crack that goes up the left side of the Southwest Buttress.

PITCH 1: Climb the Abject Cathexis crack about 40 feet, then traverse right into the excellent fingertip crack that separates the Southwest Buttress from the main Tower. Protection is excellent and the crux is near the top. Belay at the bolts (80 feet, 5.12a). **FINISH:** Rappel from the bolts. One 165-foot rope doubled will reach the bottom ledge.

SUGGESTED EQUIPMENT: No recommendation was given by first-ascent climbers.

NOTE: Bill Hatcher says, "The route is possibly the best thin fingertips route on the Tower, despite its length. The route is highly recommended and is an ideal direct start for Object Cathexis" (Route 128).

128. OBJECT CATHEXIS II or III, 5.12b

FIRST ASCENT: September 29, 1981, by Steve Hong and Mark Sonnenfeld. **APPROACH:** Take the Durrance Approach until you are on top of the Southwest Shoulder and below the Southwest Buttress. Climb to the base of Accident

Victim (Route 129) above you to set up a belay. This crack is the one that leads to the right side of the high point on the Southwest Buttress.

PITCH 1: Same as Accident Victim, Pitch 1. Climb this easy crack to the large column top belay ledge in a corner below the high point of the Southwest Buttress (120 feet, 5.6). **PITCH 2:** Face climb up to the base of a prominent diagonal crack angling left (5.10 –). Continue up the crack (just left of Accident Victim) 125 feet and traverse back right where the crack deteriorates (crux) to the belay at the top of Pitch 2 of Accident Victim (155 feet, 5.12b). **FINISH:** Rappel down or use Accident Victim to Direct Southwest (Route 130) to gain the summit. Grade II if you rappel and III if you continue to the top.

SUGGESTED EQUIPMENT: Three #1 and three #2 Friends, three sets of medium RPs, and two sets of medium Stoppers (25 pieces).

NOTE: Steve Hong gives this a one-star rating on a scale of one to three.

129. ACCIDENT VICTIM IV, 5.12a

FIRST ASCENT: August 25, 1980, by Kim Carrigan and Steve Levin. **APPROACH:** Take the Durrance Approach until you are on the Southwest Shoulder directly below the small buttress. The route starts at the base of the small buttress five columns left of Direct Southwest (Route 130).

PITCH 1: Climb up this easy corner crack to a belay ledge on the buttress top (120 feet, 5.6). **PITCH 2:** Climb up the leftward-leaning flake, then step right into the main line. Hard stemming leads to thin fingers, then hands to a good belay ledge on your left (147 feet, 5.12a). **PITCH 3:** Climb up this corner about 33 feet to a ledge on your right. Continue up and right around the next column past scary moves under a small roof and to the right, crossing three columns with poor protection to a good flake belay (85 feet, 5.11a). **PITCH 4:** Traverse up and right one crack, which puts you just above and left of a large roof. Climb up a thin crack a short way then traverse left one crack and set up a belay where the crack curves to the left (160 feet, 5.9). This pitch can also be done straight up the Direct Southwest crack (150 feet, 5.10). **FINISH:** Same as Direct Southwest Finish (70 feet, 5.6).

SUGGESTED EQUIPMENT: Full set of Hexentrics, small to medium Stoppers, and lots of wired nuts. Five sets of RPs were used by first ascent team.

NOTE: Climber Dennis Horning reports that Mark Hudon (leader) and Max Jones actually climbed Pitch 2 free prior to the reported party listed above. Government records do not show this, but Dennis could be correct.

130. DIRECT SOUTHWEST III, 5.11b

FIRST ASCENT: July 1, 1962, by John Evans and Dick Long (IV, 5.9, A3). **FIRST FREE ASCENT:** July 17, 1978, by Henry Barber and Ajax Greene. **APPROACH:** Take the Durrance Approach until you are on the Southwest Shoulder and on the right side of the base of the prominent Southwest Buttress.

PITCH 1: Climb the right crack to the top of the buttress and belay at the upper right bolts (75 feet, 5.7). **PITCH 2:** Climb the large finger crack leading up the left side of a broken column to its top. Belay at the bolts here (90 feet, 5.11b). **PITCH 3:** Climb the left crack past a bush to a ledge on the left. Traverse right across the face to a crack above and left of the large roofs. Climb up, traverse back left, and

Opposite: West Face (left) and Southwest Face

133
135
130
137
130
131
132
133
134
135
136

move up a short distance to belay (150 feet, 5.9). The original aid climb went straight up without a traverse right. **FINISH:** Climb the crack to the summit (70 feet, 5.6).

SUGGESTED EQUIPMENT: A set of Stoppers with extra small to large sizes, and a set of Hexentrics with extra #4s.

131. RANGERS ARE PEOPLE TOO I, 5.9−

FIRST ASCENT: June 14, 1985, by Jim Schlinkmann, Steve Gardiner, and Dick Guilmette. **APPROACH:** Follow the Durrance Approach until you are on top of the Southwest Shoulder and below the Southwest Buttress. The route follows the right side of the buttress (right-facing dihedral) and is one crack right of Pitch 1 of Direct Southwest (Route 130).

PITCH 1: Climb the moderate, low-angle finger crack that leads through two bushes for 70 feet (5.4). Continue up the steep portion with fingerlocks, liebacks, and stemming moves (120 feet, 5.9−). **FINISH:** Rappel from the bolts.

SUGGESTED EQUIPMENT: Small to medium Hexentrics, medium to large Stoppers, and #1 and #2 Friends.

NOTE: This is an enjoyable pitch with excellent protection.

Southwest Face

132. ACROPHOBIA IV, 5.7, A2+

FIRST ASCENT: June 22, 1980, by Steve Gardiner and Mark Brackin. **APPROACH:** Follow the Durrance Approach until just around the corner from Direct Southwest, Route 130 (one crack left of Butterfingers, Route 133, or three right of Direct Southwest), then scramble to a good belay.

PITCH 1: Aid up the thin but widening crack in the right-facing dihedral to a hanging belay (150 feet, A2). **PITCH 2:** Continue up the crack and set up a belay on top of a column on the left (75 feet, A1). **PITCH 3:** Climb the same crack until it ends, then traverse to the right under two roofs into Butterfingers (Route 133). Set up a hanging belay 20 feet above the roof (150 feet, A2+). This section is flaring and full of rotten rock. **PITCH 4:** Continue up the flaring crack on aid to a good belay marked by a fixed standard angle (75 feet, A2). **FINISH:** Climb the squeeze chimney and blocks to the summit (120 feet, 5.7).

SUGGESTED EQUIPMENT: Bugaboos, Lost Arrows, baby angles, angles, and a full set each of Stoppers and Hexentrics.

133. BUTTERFINGERS IV, 5.7, A2

FIRST ASCENT: July 15, 1979, by Steve Gardiner and Mark Brackin. **APPROACH:** Follow the Durrance Approach onto the Southwest Shoulder. Proceed just past the Southwest Buttress. The route lies four cracks right of the base of Direct Southwest (Route 130) and bisects the right half of a double roof 250 feet up.

136. GRAEME'S LINE II, 5.12b

FIRST ASCENT: As Runner's World, August 16, 1979, by Frank Sanders and Steve Gardiner (IV, 5.6, A3). **FIRST FREE ASCENT:** August 1, 1985, by Todd Skinner, Bill Hatcher, and Beth Wald. **APPROACH:** Use the Durrance Approach to the middle of the Southwest Shoulder and climb up to the base of the crack that leads to the only column-top ledge in the middle of the Southwest Face. This is on the aid route Runner's World (Route 137).

PITCH 1: Climb this thin crack, utilizing many face flaws on good protection. Utilize both cracks left of the Runner's World Column. The crux of the climb is about 130 feet up near the end of the pitch. Climb through this on the right arête to a large column-top ledge and belay here at the bolts (150 feet, 5.12b). **PITCH 2:** Continue up on stemming moves in this box to a hanging belay from bolts at the end of the crack (85 feet, 5.11). Protection is fair and the crux of the pitch is the last 25 feet. **FINISH:** Rappel down (recommended) or continue up Runner's World with aid.

SUGGESTED EQUIPMENT: Three sets of #2 to #5 RPs and many small to medium wired Stoppers. Also six quick draws and a #1/2 and a #1 Friend.

NOTE: This is a three-star route that offers steep face climbing and balance rests on the right arête near the end. According to Todd Skinner, it should become a classic. The route was named in memory of Graeme Aimer, who died tragically in 1984 in the New Zealand Alps. Six fixed pitons are in Pitch 1 and one piton is in Pitch 2.

137. RUNNER'S WORLD IV, 5.6, A3 (5.12b free)

FIRST ASCENT: August 16, 1979, by Frank Sanders and Steve Gardiner. **APPROACH:** Use the Durrance Approach to the middle of the Southwest Shoulder and climb up to the base of the cracks that lead to the only column-top ledge in the middle of the Southwest Face.

PITCH 1: This has been climbed free as Graeme's Line, Route 136 (150 feet, 5.12b). **PITCH 2:** This has been climbed free as Graeme's Line (85 feet, 5.11). **PITCH 3:** Get into the left crack and climb until an obvious ledge can take you right. The ledge is well-defined but has a poor bolt in the middle. Traverse to Centennial, Route 138 (130 feet, A2). Use lots of knifeblades, Lost Arrows, and bugaboos. **FINISH:** Same as Centennial Finish (100 feet, 5.6, A3).

SUGGESTED EQUIPMENT: See Graeme's Line for the free portion. Take extra bugaboos and Lost Arrows, plus lots of knifeblades, as two pitches are very thin.

NOTE: Anchors and belays are excellent, but the top pitch is a bit loose. Have a good time. You've got to bop until you drop.

138. CENTENNIAL III, A3

FIRST ASCENT: June 10, 1978, by Terry Rypkema, Frank Sanders, and Steve Gardiner. **APPROACH:** Follow the Durrance Approach to the middle of the Southwest Face. Pass Zephyr (Route 135) and Runner's World (Route 137). Centennial is several cracks right of Runner's World and about 14 cracks left of Romeo Is Restless (Route 141). Start climbing in a shallow, right-facing dihedral two cracks to the right of a broken-off column.

Southwest Face

PITCH 1: Aid this narrow crack to the end of your rope (165 feet, A2+). The crack widens a little the last few feet so you can set up a solid, hanging belay with large angles. **PITCH 2:** Continue up the same crack until a traverse to the next crack right is feasible. Climb this crack on aid until you are just beneath an overhang where flaky rock necessitates a leftward traverse across a horizontal crack. Better pins lead up to a good belay with a poor attempt at a bolt above the overhang (165 feet, A2). **PITCH 3:** Continue up until a secure hanging belay can be established in a horizontal crack to the left, just below a leftward arch (100 feet, 5.6, A3). Varied and interesting aid problems characterize this pitch because the nature of the rock is continually changing. **FINISH:** Climb the arch to the summit (100 feet, A3).

SUGGESTED EQUIPMENT: Lots of blades and small angles. The upper pitches use many large pieces.

NOTE: This is an excellent climb — long and sustained — which offers secure belays, varied problems, and spectacular views. It has the distinction of being the only climb on the Tower with no free moves.

139. UNKNOWN ROUTE LEFT Aid

EXPLANATION: This route is clearly marked on the park's large route photo showing the east end of the Southwest Face. It may be an aid route done by Frank Sanders in the late seventies or early eighties. Lying between Centennial (Route 138) and Romeo Is Restless (Route 141), it is closer to Centennial. The line goes up a long crack that passes between a double roof on the left and a single roof on the right at the same level partway up the face. A little farther up, it passes another roof immediately on its right side and then continues up to the summit in the obvious crack above.

SUGGESTED EQUIPMENT: Large aid rack with a few larger pieces for the top. Small to medium pieces should do most of the route.

NOTE: Just to the right of this crack is Unknown Route Right (Route 140), which does not go to the summit.

140. UNKNOWN ROUTE RIGHT Aid

EXPLANATION: This route is clearly marked on the park's large route photo showing the east end of the Southwest Face, but the date of the first ascent is not known. It lies between Centennial (Route 138) and Romeo Is Restless (Route 141) but is closer to Romeo Is Restless (about six cracks to its left). The photo shows the route continuing up to a point where the crack seems to close off at about the height of a large roof on the left. From this point climb a few feet and traverse left to the crack that passed the left roof on the right side. Continue up this crack to another large roof directly above you and pass it on the left. Climb up a short distance and then traverse right to a good crack between and above two roofs. From here you can rappel off as the original unknown climbers did or you can climb the easier-appearing crack above you to the summit.

SUGGESTED EQUIPMENT: Lots of small to medium pieces and a few larger ones, especially if you are going to the top.

NOTE: If you have any information on this or other routes that we do not have, please write Superintendent; Devils Tower National Monument; Devils Tower, Wyoming 82714.

141. ROMEO IS RESTLESS I, 5.12b

FIRST ASCENT: As Tower Direct (Route 142), November 2, 1975, by Pat Padden and Rodney Johnson (III, 5.8, A2). **FIRST FREE ASCENT:** July 22, 1985, by Todd Skinner and Beth Wald. **APPROACH:** Follow the Durrance Approach to the base of Tower Direct. Scramble up and left to a small ledge below the route to start. This is on the aid route Tower Direct and leads up to the lowest of five connected large roofs.

PITCH 1: Climb up this desperately thin crack with powerful but delicate climbing. The crux is face climbing about halfway up the pitch. The crack widens eventually to a fist crack. There is a lot of 5.11 climbing and fair protection. Climb to a very unusual sitting belay at the bolts on a ledge below the roof (150 feet, 5.12b). **FINISH:** Rappel down (recommended) or Todd Skinner says free climbing to the summit would be possible but dirty. To continue to the top, follow the Tower Direct aid route.

SUGGESTED EQUIPMENT: Four to five sets of #3, #4, and #5 RPs, some small and medium wired Stoppers, two each #3 and #3-1/2 Friends, and one each #2, #2-1/2, and #4 Friends.

NOTE: Save one #3 RP for the last moves.

142. TOWER DIRECT III, 5.8, A2 (5.12b free)

FIRST ASCENT: November 2, 1975, by Pat Padden and Rodney Johnson. **FIRST FREE ASCENT:** of Pitch 1 only — July 22, 1985, by Todd Skinner and Beth Wald. **APPROACH:** Walk the Durrance Approach until you are almost at the Leaning Column (Route 1), then traverse left and set up a belay. The route is the crack that runs up directly under the middle and lowest of five large roofs.

PITCH 1: This pitch has been climbed free as Romeo Is Restless (Route 141) (150 feet, 5.12b). **PITCH 2:** Free climb with some aid up to the overhang and pass it on the left. Climb directly up to and over the next overhang. Continue up 50 feet to a belay stance (140 feet, A1 or A2). **PITCH 3:** Free climb the crack above you to a good belay stance (130 feet, 5.8). **FINISH:** Free climb over an overhang and to the top (100 feet, 5.7).

SUGGESTED EQUIPMENT: Set each of Hexentrics and Stoppers, lots of small nuts and Stoppers. Runners and Friends are helpful. See Romeo Is Restless for equipment for freeing Pitch 1.

NOTE: Pitch 1 was originally done with many pitons (horizontals, angles, and bongs).

143. POTC II, 5.10d

FIRST ASCENT: August 24, 1965, by Pete Oslund and Tom Christensen (III, 5.7, A3). **FIRST FREE ASCENT:** June 4, 1978, by Frank Sanders and Dennis Horning. **APPROACH:** Use the Durrance Approach. The route lies three cracks left of the Leaning Column (Route 1).

PITCH 1: Climb up the crack and belay below the roof (160 feet, 5.10d). **PITCH 2:** Climb up and over the left side of the roof to an off-width crack and chimney above. Belay on the column top (160 feet, 5.10b). **FINISH:** Traverse right and climb up to the Bailey Direct Finish (Route 4) to Durrance (Route 1). Climb this and belay at the Durrance rappel bolts (150 feet, 5.5). You can also traverse right to the Meadows and reach the summit by the Standard Meadows Finish.

SUGGESTED EQUIPMENT: Full set each of Stoppers and Hexentrics with extra medium to large Stoppers. Take extra #5 to #12 Stoppers and 2- to 5-inch pieces.

NOTE: Initials stand for the names of the first-ascent climbers.

144. BLACK-JONES DIRECT II, 5.11b

FIRST ASCENT: Exact date and climbers unknown, but was climbed on aid prior to the establishment of Manifest Destiny, Route 145 (see Note below). **FIRST FREE ASCENT:** July ?, 1979, by Steve Jones and Carol Black. **APPROACH:** Follow the Durrance Approach to the base of the Leaning Column (Route 1). The route starts one crack right of POTC (Route 143) and two cracks left of the base of the Leaning Column.

PITCH 1: Climb up this thin crack until Manifest Destiny (Route 145) joins it. Continue up a little farther to the belay/rappel bolts on your left (155 feet, 5.11b). **FINISH:** Rappel off or continue up on Manifest Destiny and take any of several options to reach the summit.

SUGGESTED EQUIPMENT: Lots of small pieces. See Manifest Destiny for equipment if you plan to go higher.

NOTE: Elvin (Al) Aaberg, former chief ranger at Devils Tower, said he spent a day watching some climbers aid up the crack (bottom to top) that starts at the base of Black-Jones Direct, then climb through what is now the end of Pitch 1 and all of Pitch 2 of Manifest Destiny before that route was put up. The climbers and date are not known and no park record can be found. — Dick Guilmette

145. MANIFEST DESTINY III, 5.9−

FIRST ASCENT: See Note, Black-Jones Direct (Route 144). **FIRST FREE ASCENT:** August 21, 1973, by Bruce Bright and Dennis Drayna. **APPROACH:** Follow the Durrance Approach to the base of the Leaning Column (Route 1). The route starts one crack right of Black-Jones Direct (Route 144) and one crack left of the Leaning Column.

PITCH 1: Follow the ever-widening, extremely steep crack (fingers and fist) until the crack turns left and you can join the main crack on your left. Continue up this crack to a hanging belay at the bolts on your left (155 feet, 5.9−). **PITCH 2:** Continue up this increasingly large crack chimney to the column tops for a belay (120 feet, 5.8). **FINISH:** Follow the chimney above the climb to the summit (150 feet, 5.6). You can also traverse right to the Meadows for a Standard Meadows Finish or do the Bailey Direct (Route 4).

SUGGESTED EQUIPMENT: A full rack plus a number of large pieces (to 4 inches) and runners.

NOTE: See Black-Jones Direct.

APPENDIX

Climbing History

DATE	ROUTES, CLIMBS, PITCHES	GRADE/ RATING	PIONEERED BY
6-28-1937	Wiessner	II, 5.7	Fritz Wiessner, William House, Lawrence Coveny
9-8-1938	Durrance	II, 5.6	Jack Durrance, Harrison Butterworth
7-2-1948	Conn Traverse	5.5	Herb Conn, Jan Conn
8-30-1951	Soler First Free Ascent 5-2-1959	II, Aid	Anton (Tony) Soler, Art Lembeck, Herb Conn, Ray Moore, Chris Scordus
8-10-1954	Pseudo-Wiessner	II, 5.8	Ray Northcutt, Harvey T. Carter
7-26-1955	McCarthy West Face First Free Ascent 8-11-1979	IV, 5.8, A3	Jim McCarthy, John Rupley
6-7-1956	Casper College First Free Ascent 6-1-1979	III, 5.7, A2	Dud McReynolds, Walt Bailey, David Sturdevant, Bruce Smith
7-9-1956	M&CWTC #1 (Devils Delight) First Free Ascent 7-2-1962	II, Aid	Cecil Ouellette, Charles Kness
7-10-1956	M&CWTC #2 (TAD) First Free Ascent 7-3-1973	II, Aid	Dale Gallagher, Jack Morehead
7-12-1956	M&CWTC #3	II, Aid	Cecil Ouellette, Charles Kness
7-14-1956	M&CWTC #4	II, Aid	Marcus Russi, John Callahan
7-16-1956	M&CWTC #5	II, Aid	Exact Army Climbers Unknown
8-5-1957	McCarthy North Face First Free Ascent 5-28-1978	III, 5.7, A2	Jim McCarthy, John Rupley
2-2-1958	Bailey Direct (of Durrance)	II, 5.5	Walt Bailey, Raymond Jacquot, Jim Kothel, Richard Williams, Kenneth Johnson
8-17-1958	Sundance	II, 5.7	Bob Kamps, Dave Rearick, Verena Frymann
8-20-1958	Bon Homme	II, 5.9	Bob Kamps, Don Yestness
5-2-1959	First Free Ascent of Soler	II, 5.9−	Layton Kor, Raymond Jacquot
7-23-1959	Gooseberry Jam	III, 5.9−	Bob Kamps, Don Yestness
7-26-1959	Walt Bailey Memorial First Free Ascent 5-27-1974	II, 5.8, A2	Gary Cole, Raymond Jacquot, Charles Blackmon
5-8-1960	Hollywood and Vine First Free Ascent 5-26-1974	III, 5.5, A1	Gary Cole, Raymond Jacquot
5-13-1961	Vulture First Free Ascent 7-9-1985	IV, 5.8, A3	Layton Kor, Bob LaGrange

Opposite: Jim Schlinkmann leading first ascent of Rangers Are People Too (Route 131), 1985 (Dick Guilmette photo)

DATE	ROUTES, CLIMBS, PITCHES	GRADE/ RATING	PIONEERED BY
5-28-1961	Belle Fourche Buttress First Free Ascent 10-16-1977	III, 5.8, A3	Don Ryan, Gary Cole
7-16-1961	Northwest Corner	5.8+, A3	Layton Kor, Herb Swedlund
7-1-1962	Direct Southwest First Free Ascent 7-17-1978	IV, 5.9, A3	John Evans, Dick Long
7-2-1962	Devils Delight (First Free Ascent of M&CWTC #1)	II, 5.8+	John Evans, Dennis Becker
4-26-1964	Saber First Free Ascent 8-22-1985	IV, 5.6, A3	Layton Kor, Floyd Tex Bossier
5-3-1964	Conquistador	IV, 5.7, A3	Floyd Tex Bossier, Steve Komito
6-2-1964	Northeast Corner	III, 5.7, A3	Dean Moore, Paul Stettner
8-19-1964	Danse Macabre	II, 5.10d	Royal Robbins, Peter Robinson
8-20-1964	The Window	IV, 5.6, A4	Royal Robbins, Peter Robinson
10-31-1964	Delta I First Free Ascent 9-15-1976	II, 5.8, A2	Bob Schlichting, Bill Heatley
5-1-1965	Direct Southeast First Free Ascent 8-24-1978	II, 5.5, A2	Peter Oslund, John Horn
8-24-1965	POTC First Free Ascent 6-4-1978	III, 5.7, A3	Pete Oslund, Tom Christensen
8-26-1965	Cave First Free Ascent 9-20-1976	II, 5.5, A2	Pete Oslund, Dave Ingalls
9-4-1967	The D.O.M. (Dirty Old Man)	II, A2 or A3	Ron Howe, Terry O'Donnell, Evans Winner
9-24-1967	El Matador First Free Ascent 8-6-1978	IV, 5.7, A3	Fred Beckey, Eric Bjornstad
7-6-1968	Exit-US First Free Ascent 9-27-1976	II, 5.5, A2	Dave Ingalls, Roy Kligfield
10-6-1968	Second Cave (Last Cowgirl Camp) First Free Ascent 8-27-1979	II, 5.7, A2	Pete Oslund, John Chuta
7-24-1969	The Route of All Evil (Dr. Zen) First Free Ascent 9-1-1983	III, 5.8, A3	David Lunn, John Luz, Bruce Morris
10-18-1970	B. O. Plenty First Free Ascent 9-16-1976	III, A2	Charles Bare, Jim Olson
4-22-1971	Troglodytes Trauma First Free Ascent 6-14-1979	II, A3	Ian Wade, Barbara Euser, Walter Fricke
5-8-1971	Patent Pending First Free Ascent 8-17-1972	III, 5.7, A1 or A2	Charles Bare, Jim Olson
6-2-1972	Tulgey Wood	III, 5.10a	Mark Hesse, Dan McClure
7-10-1972	Carpenter's Caper	II, 5.7, A2	Terry Rypkema, Roger Holtorf, Bruce Bright
8-17-1972	First Free Ascent of Patent Pending	III, 5.8+	Bruce Bright, Dennis Drayna
9-14-1972	Uncle Remus Dirty Vegetable Garden	II, 5.4, A2	Mike Brown, Frank Sanders
11-5-1972	Bon Homme, Horning Variation	II, 5.8	Dennis Horning, Howard Hauck

DATE	ROUTES, CLIMBS, PITCHES	GRADE/ RATING	PIONEERED BY
7-3-1973	TAD First Free Ascent of M&CWTC #2	II, 5.7	Dan Burgette, Charles Bare
8-10-1973	Conquest of Tillie's Lookout (Brokedown Palace) First Free Ascent 10-2-1981	III, 5.8, A2	Bruce Price, Mike LaLone
8-21-1973	Manifest Destiny	III, 5.9−	Bruce Bright, Dennis Drayna
10-21-1973	El Cracko Diablo	II, 5.8	Rod Johnson, Pat Padden
5-26-1974	First Free Ascent of Hollywood and Vine	II, 5.10c	Jeff Overton, Scott Woodruff
5-27-1974	First Free Ascent of Walt Bailey Memorial	II, 5.9	Jeff Overton, Scott Woodruff
6-2-1974	Suchness First Free Ascent 9-7-1976	III, 5.8, A1	Dennis Horning, Paul Piana
9-8-1974	Devils Delight—Direct	I, 5.7	Dennis Horning, Judd Jennerjahn, Rob Wheeler
5-18-1975	Assembly Line	III, 5.9	Dennis Horning, Judd Jennerjahn
8-31-1975	Sunfighter	II, 5.8+	Dennis Horning, Jim Slichter
8-31-1975	Witchie	III, 5.10a	Geoffrey Conley, John Pearson
11-2-1975	Tower Direct First Free Ascent 7-22-1985 (Pitch 1)	III, 5.8, A2	Pat Padden, Rodney Johnson
5-1-1976	Todtmoos	II, 5.9−	Dennis Horning, Jim Slichter
5-31-1976	Waterfall	II, 5.9−	Dennis Horning, Skip Fossen, Mark Santangelo
6-9-1976	Journey to Ixtlan	II, 5.10b	Dennis Horning, Perry Ohlsen
7-2-1976	Crocodile	III, 5.10d	Dennis Horning, Curt Haire
7-7-1976	McCarthy West Face, Heads Up Variation	I, 5.10a	Greg Newth, Dave Hoag
7-30-1976	Mr. Clean First Free Ascent 8-14-1977	III, 5.10, A1	Curt Haire, Dennis Horning
9-7-1976	First Free Ascent of Suchness	III, 5.10b	Dennis Horning, Frank Sanders
9-15-1976	First Free Ascent of Delta I	II, 5.9−	Dennis Horning, Frank Sanders
9-16-1976	First Free Ascent of B. O. Plenty	II, 5.9−	Frank Sanders, Dennis Horning
9-20-1976	First Free Ascent of Cave	II, 5.9	Dennis Horning, Frank Sanders
9-24-1976	Beelzebub	II, 5.10b	Dennis Horning, Frank Sanders
9-27-1976	First Free Ascent of Exit-US	II, 5.9	Frank Sanders, Dennis Horning
9-28-1976	Kama Sutra	III, 5.10a	Dennis Horning, Cody Paulson, Frank Sanders
6-15-1977	One-Way Sunset	III, 5.10c	Dennis Horning, Jim Slichter
6-25-1977	Extended Wiessner	I, 5.8	Unknown
8-14-1977	First Free Ascent of Mr. Clean	III, 5.11a	Henry Barber, Chip Lee
9-25-1977	Bittersweet	II, 5.10c	Dennis Horning, Frank Sanders
9-28-1977	Second Thought, Bon Homme Variation	II, 5.7	Dennis Horning, Howard Hauck
10-12-1977	Non-Dairy Creamer (Bloodguard) First Free Ascent 7-19-1984 (Pitch 1)	III, 5.8, A3	Chris Ballinger, Jim Lynch, Frank Sanders
10-16-1977	First Free Ascent of Belle Fourche Buttress	III, 5.10b	Dennis Horning, Dave Rasmussen

DATE	ROUTES, CLIMBS, PITCHES	GRADE/ RATING	PIONEERED BY
10-25-1977	Made for Aid (Digital Extraction) First Free Ascent 5-19-1982	III, 5.8, A3	Keith Lober (solo)
10-30-1977	Burning Daylight	II, 5.10b	Dennis Horning, Mike Todd
4-2-1978	Afternoon Delight (The Power that Preserves) First Free Ascent 7-12-1983	II, A2	Terry Rypkema, Frank Sanders
5-13-1978	Maid in the Shaid First Free Ascent 6-25-1983	III, 5.8, A2	Terry Rypkema, Frank Sanders, Steve Gardiner, Debbie Bergland
5-14-1978	Speedway (English Beat) First Free Ascent 7-22-1984	II, A3	Terry Rypkema, Steve Gardiner
5-28-1978	First Free Ascent of McCarthy North Face	III, 5.11a	Dennis Horning, Frank Sanders
5-?-1978	Gooseberry Jam, Peterson Variation	III, 5.10a	Don Peterson
6-4-1978	First Free Ascent of POTC	II, 5.10d	Frank Sanders, Dennis Horning
6-10-1978	Centennial	III, A3	Terry Rypkema, Frank Sanders, Steve Gardiner
7-1-1978	McCarthy West Face, Free Variation	II, 5.10b	Chris Ballinger, Dennis Horning, Steve Gardiner
7-17-1978	First Free Ascent of Direct Southwest	III, 5.11b	Henry Barber, Ajax Greene
7-22-1978	Phillip's Retreat	I, 5.9+	Dennis Horning, Phillip Chandler-belay
7-27-1978	Two Left Shoes	III, 5.8, A1	Jim Beyer (solo)
8-6-1978	First Free Ascent of El Matador	III, 5.10d	Bob Yoho, Chick Holtkamp
8-19-1978	Carol's Crack	III, 5.11a	Bob Yoho, Carol Black, Chick Holtkamp, Jeff Baird
8-24-1978	First Free Ascent of Direct Southeast	II, 5.11d	Steve Hong, Mark Smedley, Karin Budding
10-21-1978	Tower Classic (Let Me Go Wild) First Free Ascent 8-15-1984	III, 5.7, A2	Steve Gardiner, Terry Rypkema, Frank Sanders
10-29-1978	Lucifer's Ledges	III, A3	Frank Sanders, Steve Gardiner, Terry Rypkema, Mark Brackin
5-11-1979	McCarthy West Face, Hong Variation	I, 5.11c	Steve Hong, Karin Budding
6-1-1979	First Free Ascent of Casper College	III, 5.10d	Jim Beyer, Dennis Horning
6-1-1979	Morchella Esculenta First Free Ascent 9-6-1980	II, 5.7, A3	Larry Wydra, Tom Ptacek
6-9-1979	Zephyr	III, 5.9, A1	Jim Beyer (solo)
6-14-1979	First Free Ascent of Troglodytes Trauma	II, 5.11c	Jim Beyer, Dennis Horning
7-?-1979	Black-Jones Direct	II, 5.11b	Steve Jones, Carol Black
7-15-1979	Butterfingers	IV, 5.7, A2	Steve Gardiner, Mark Brackin
7-30-1979	Path of Dissent	II, 5.9	Mark Smedley, Jim Black, Rich Jaskiewiez
8-11-1979	First Free Ascent of McCarthy West Face	III, 5.11c	Steve Hong, Karin Budding
8-16-1979	Runner's World (Graeme's Line) First Free Ascent 8-1-1985 (2 pitches)	IV, 5.6, A3	Frank Sanders, Steve Gardiner

DATE	ROUTES, CLIMBS, PITCHES	GRADE/ RATING	PIONEERED BY
8-27-1979	Last Cowgirl Camp First Free Ascent of Second Cave	II, 5.11b	Dennis Horning, Jay Smith
5-17-1980	Persistence	II, 5.9	Steve Gardiner, Frank Sanders
5-24-1980	Double Indemnity	II, 5.11a	Steve Hong, Karin Budding, Mark Smedley
5-25-1980	Four Play	III, 5.11c	Steve Hong, Karin Budding, Mark Smedley, Bill Feiges
6-1-1980	Misty Morning Melody	II, 5.8, A2	Steve Gardiner, Frank Sanders, Mark Brackin
6-22-1980	Acrophobia	IV, 5.7, A2+	Steve Gardiner, Mark Brackin
7-4-1980	Independence	III, 5.8, A3	Frank Sanders (solo)
8-25-1980	Accident Victim	IV, 5.12a	Kim Carrigan, Steve Levin
9-6-1980	First Free Ascent of Morchella Esculenta	II, 5.11c	Dennis Horning, Mark Smedley
9-7-1980	Blade City	IV, A3+	Frank Sanders, Steve Gardiner
9-13-1980	The Thin Dagger	IV, A2	Don Grady, Rod Johnson
9-20-1980	Let Me Go Wild First Free Ascent of Tower Classic (Pitch 1)	II, 5.12b	Mark Smedley, Jim Black
5-21-1981	Emotional Rescue	III, 5.7, A3+	Frank Sanders, Chris Engle
5-29-1981	Gimme Shelter, Variation Emotional Rescue	III, 5.7, A3	Frank Sanders (solo)
6-30-1981	Way Layed	I, 5.11b	Eric Rhicard, Mark Smedley
8-29-1981	Dump Watt	II, 5.10b	Mark Smedley, Dave Larsen, Eric Rhicard
8-29-1981	Jumpin' Jack Flash First Free Ascent 6-18-85 (Pitches 2 & 3) First Free Ascent 8-3-85 (Pitch 1)	III, 5.7, A2	Frank Sanders, Dale Chamberlain (as Daredevil Index) (as Leaping Lizards)
9-5-1981	Sympathy for the Devil First Free Ascent 6-27-82 (Pitch 2) First Free Ascent 8-6-85 (Pitch 3)	III, 5.9, A2	Frank Sanders, Chris Engle
9-29-1981	Object Cathexis (variation of Accident Victim)	II or III, 5.12b	Steve Hong, Mark Sonnenfeld
10-2-1981	Brokedown Palace First Free Ascent of Conquest of Tillie's Lookout	III, 5.12b	Steve Hong, Mark Sonnenfeld
3-?-1982	Seamstress First Free Ascent 6-?-1982	II, A2	Chris Engle, Dave Johnson
5-19-1982	Digital Extraction First Free Ascent of Made for Aid	III, 5.11d	Steve Hong, Mark Sonnenfeld
6-?-1982	First Free Ascent of Seamstress	II, 5.12c	Steve Hong, Karin Budding
6-10-1982	New Wave	I, 5.10a	Dave Larsen, Dennis Horning
6-22-1982	Broken Tree	I, 5.10b	Dennis Horning, Dave Larsen
6-27-1982	Back to Montana First Free Ascent of Sympathy for the Devil (Pitch 2)	II, 5.10d	Dennis Horning, Monte Cooper
7-11-1982	The Chute	I, 5.10d	Dennis Horning, Hollis Marriott
5-27-1983	Abject Cathexis	III, A3	Eric Breitenberger, William Trull
6-4-1983	Adventurous Daze	IV, 5.10a, A2 or A3	Frank Sanders, Chris Engle

DATE	ROUTES, CLIMBS, PITCHES	GRADE/ RATING	P
6-25-1983	First Free Ascent of Maid in the Shaid	III, 5.11d	Bu
6-26-1983	Deli Express	II, 5.12a	Mark S
6-27-1983	A Bridge Too Far	I, 5.11d	Todd Ski, Steve Hong
7-12-1983	The Power that Preserves First Free Ascent of Afternoon Delight	II, 5.12a	Todd Skinner, Moana Roberts (jumarred)
7-14-1983	Synchronicity	I, 5.11d	Todd Skinner, John Rosholt
7-24-1983	Two Moons over Hulett (parts of this route follow Emotional Rescue)	II, 5.11b	Dennis Horning, Dave Larsen
8-13-1983	Everlasting	I, 5.10c	Dennis Horning, Dave Larsen
8-15-1983	Klondike	I, 5.10a	Dave Larsen, Dennis Horning
9-1-1983	Dr. Zen First Free Ascent of The Route of All Evil	III, 5.11c	Steve Mankenberg, Dave Larsen
4-14-1984	Pigeon English	II, 5.9–	Paul Piana, Bill Hatcher
7-2-1984	Mateo Tepee	II, 5.7, A3	Steve Gardiner, Joe Sears
7-4-1984	Satan's Stairway	III, 5.8, A3	Steve Gardiner, Joe Sears, Chris Engle, Dave Johnson
7-14-1984	Surfer Girl (partly on M&CWTC aid route)	II, 5.12c	Todd Skinner, Beth Wald
7-19-1984	Approaching Lavender	II, 5.11c	Paul Piana, Bob Cowan, Todd Skinner, Beth Wald
7-19-1984	Bloodguard First Free Ascent of Non-Dairy Creamer (Pitch 1)	I, 5.12a	Todd Skinner, Beth Wald, Bob Cowan, Paul Piana
7-20-1984	The Best Crack in Minnesota	I, 5.9	Paul Piana, Bob Cowan, Todd Skinner, Beth Wald
7-22-1984	English Beat First Free Ascent of Speedway	II, 5.12b	Todd Skinner, Paul Piana, Bob Cowan, Frank Hill, Kevin Lindorff
7-26-1984	Avalon	II, 5.11d	Todd Skinner, Beth Wald
8-1-1984	Animal Cracker Land	I, 5.12b	Todd Skinner, Beth Wald
8-15-1984	Let Me Go Wild First Free Ascent of Tower Classic (Pitch 2)	II, 5.12b	Todd Skinner, Beth Wald
8-15-1984	Psychic Turbulence	I, 5.11a	Todd Skinner, Daniel Rosen, Beth Wald
6-14-1985	Rangers Are People Too	I, 5.9–	Jim Schlinkmann, Steve Gardiner, Dick Guilmette
6-15-1985	McCarthy's Brother	II, 5.10a	Dennis Horning, Jim Schlinkmann
6-18-1985	Daredevil Index First Free Ascent of Jumpin' Jack Flash (Pitches 2 & 3)	III, 5.12a	Paul Piana, Steve Petro
7-7-1985	NAM	I, 5.8	Dick Guilmette, Bruce Adams
7-9-1985	First Free Ascent of Vulture	IV, 5.12a	Steve Hong, Karin Budding, Beth Wald
7-10-1985	Potatoes Alien	I, 5.10b	Mateo Pee Pee, "Barney" Fisher, Jim Schlinkmann
7-16-1985	No Holds for Bonzo First Free Ascent of NAM	I, 5.11b	Mateo Pee Pee, Jim Schlinkmann
7-17-1985	Raindance	I, 5.10a	Carl Coy, Beth Wald
7-18-1985	Spiney Norman	I, 5.12b	Todd Skinner, Beth Wald

DATE	ROUTES, CLIMBS, PITCHES	GRADE/ RATING	PIONEERED BY
7-21-1985	Extension	II, 5.10d	Dennis Horning, Jim Schlinkmann
7-21-1985	Jerry's Kids	I, 5.10b	Jim Schlinkmann, Mateo Pee Pee, "Barney" Fisher
7-22-1985	Romeo Is Restless First Free Ascent of Tower Direct	I, 5.12b	Todd Skinner, Beth Wald
7-27-1985	Mystic and the Mulchers	I, 5.8–	Jim Schlinkmann, Dick Guilmette, "Barney" Fisher, Mateo Pee Pee
7-27-1985	Nitro Express	II, 5.11c	Steve Petro, Todd Skinner, Beth Wald
7-30-1985	Verrouiller Letoit Pendang La Marche	II, 5.7, A3	Kyle Copeland, John Gill
8-1-1985	Graeme's Line First Free Ascent of Runner's World	II, 5.12b	Todd Skinner, Bill Hatcher, Beth Wald
8-3-1985	Leaping Lizards First Free Ascent of Jumpin' Jack Flash (Pitch 1)	I, 5.10a	Carl Coy, Mark Jacobs
8-6-1985	Hollow Men First Free Ascent of Sympathy for the Devil (Pitch 3)	II, 5.12c	Todd Skinner, Beth Wald
8-10-1985	Risque	I, 5.12	Todd Skinner, Beth Wald, Jim Schlinkmann, Bill Hatcher
8-12-1985	Billie Bear Cranks the Rad	I, 5.12a	Bill Hatcher, Todd Skinner, Rick Erker
8-14-1985	See You in Soho	I, 5.12b	Todd Skinner, Beth Wald
8-22-1985	Spank the Monkey First Free Ascent of Saber (Pitch 1)	I, 5.11a	Jim Schlinkmann, Mateo Pee Pee, Carl Coy
8-26-1985	Neverlasting	I, 5.9–	David Kozak, Denny Hochwender
9-1-1985	White Lightning	III, A2	Mark Gordon, Kristi Rolf
9-3-1985	Buster Cattlefield	I, 5.11d	Tom Kalakay, Mal Ham, Bill Dockins, Kristen Drumheller

INDEX

Steve Gardiner

Dick Guilmette

About the authors:

Steve Gardiner, a teacher of English and journalism in Jackson, Wyoming, has made over 100 climbs on Devils Tower including 15 first ascents. He's also climbed in the Andes, Alps, Colorado Rockies, Tetons and Cascades. As a free-lance writer, Gardiner has published more than 200 articles in regional magazines and newspapers, as well as mountaineering and western history periodicals, winning 15 state press association writing awards. He is the author of *Rumblings from Razor City: The Oral History of Gillette, Wyoming.*

Dick Guilmette has daily contact with visitors to Devils Tower in his position as Chief Ranger, Devils Tower National Monument. He's well versed in the needs of climbers and visitors within the national park system, as he was a ranger at Grand Teton, Yellowstone and Denali national parks before coming to Devils Tower over six years ago. An active climber himself, Guilmette has done many of the routes on the Tower.